Autonomy and Schooling

Autonomy and Schooling

EAMONN CALLAN

McGill-Queen's University Press
Kingston and Montreal

© McGill-Queen's University Press 1988
ISBN 0-7735-0647-0

Legal deposit third quarter 1988
Bibliothèque nationale du Québec

∞

Printed in Canada on acid-free paper

This book has been published with the help of a
grant from the Social Science Federation of Canada,
using funds provided by the Social Sciences and
Humanities Research Council of Canada.

Canadian Cataloguing in Publication Data

Callan, Eamonn, 1953-
    Autonomy and schooling
    Includes bibliographical references and an index.
    ISBN 0-7735-0647-0
    1. Education — Philosophy. 2. Self-government
    (in education). I. Title.
    LB880.C34 1988   370'.1   C88-090141-1

For Corinne

Contents

Acknowledgments

I wrote this book as a Mactaggart Fellow in the Department of Educational Foundations at the University of Alberta. If I had not been fortunate enough to obtain the fellowship, the book might never have been written. I am grateful to Mr Sandy Mactaggart for his generosity in establishing the Mactaggart Fellowships. Helpful comments on an earlier draft were provided by the reader for McGill-Queen's University Press and one of the readers for the Aid to Scholarly Publications Programme. At an earlier stage in the development of my work, Allen Pearson, Ivan DeFaveri, Kenneth Strike, and especially Gerry Gaden gave me valuable guidance. For anyone familiar with the writings of P.S. Wilson and Michael Bonnett, their influence upon my thinking will be obvious, though it will be equally apparent that they would disagree with many of my arguments.

Autonomy and Schooling

Introduction

The publication of Jean Jacques Rousseau's *Emile* in 1762 initiated a controversial though somewhat ill-defined tradition in the philosophy of education, a tradition usually referred to as "child-centred education." The numerous and often outrageous educational strictures and prescriptions found in this remarkable novel are often couched in the language of liberation. Conventional forms of upbringing allegedly enslave the mind, but the radically unconventional education of Rousseau's child-protagonist is supposed to be faithful to the ideal of freedom. To be sure, Emile is hemmed in by a host of constraints as he grows up, but the point of these pervasive restrictions is to ensure that he will develop the kind of character upon which the value of freedom depends. Emile is to be educated for autonomy; he is to become someone capable of self-rule in a civilization deeply hostile to self-rule.

The twin concepts of freedom and autonomy are fundamental to the child-centred tradition as it developed after Rousseau, though they have often been used to support ideas he did not anticipate and would not have commended. The diversity of policies and practices which have been espoused in this way should not surprise us. Freedom and autonomy are highly elastic concepts, easily stretched to fit the defence of what is stupid or evil. Moreover, the reckless spirit of romanticism, which has often animated the child-centred tradition, has made the tradition acutely vulnerable to this kind of abuse. In this book I hope to show that there is rather more value in the child-centred tradition than its notorious excesses might lead one to suspect. I shall attempt to explain and defend a cluster of doctrines which are at least close to what some exponents of that tradition have advocated in the past. The structure of the argument parallels Rousseau's in that the defence of these doctrines is rooted in a certain theory of the nature and value of freedom and autonomy. This theory will be the focus of the first two chapters. The remaining chapters argue that a curriculum based upon the psychological interests of students is needed in our schools; that compulsion for the sake of educational ends is justifiable, though the scope of warranted compulsion is narrower than is commonly assumed; and that in an educationally adequate form of schooling, there is good reason to institute a democratic, or at least a quasi-democratic authority structure during its latter stages.

The idea that schooling should help students become autonomous adults is one that continues to command widespread interest and adherence among contemporary philosophers of education – even politicians and educational bureaucrats are apt to pay the notion lip service occasionally. But the child-centred doctrines I have just endorsed are another matter. Although they might receive sympathetic attention from time to time, their radical tenor is decidedly unfashionable nowadays. For instance, in the tough-minded atmosphere of contemporary educational theory and practice, the claim that schools should ever be democracies will not find a large receptive audience, even among high-minded philosophers of education. It is my contention, however, that these ideas form a coherent whole. An interest-based curriculum is justified because it contributes to autonomy. Substantial limits on the use of compulsion for educational ends must be acknowledged once we accept autonomy as a fundamental educational value. Moreover, its value also provides powerful grounds for creating democratic schooling (or something quite close to it) under certain conditions.

If autonomy as an educational ideal has these implications for schooling, those who find the implications untenable might try to evade them by rejecting the ideal or by consigning it to a peripheral position in their scheme of educational values. I shall try to foreclose this move or at least make it less attractive than it might initially seem for those hostile to the child-centred tradition. In the first place, it will be shown that autonomy is an ideal which cannot be jettisoned or de-emphasized without causing havoc to other widely and deeply held valuations about freedom, self-respect, and moral virtue. Second, it should become apparent that the policies recommended here can be endorsed without accepting other child-centred doctrines which are likely to be indefensible. At no point does my argument depend on the discredited ideas that children are naturally good (whatever that might mean); that education is aptly conceived as a process of growth; and that learning should proceed through personal discovery, with teachers providing some modest guidance along the way. In dissociating these plainly wrongheaded ideas from elements in the child-centred tradition which have enduring merit, at least some serious obstacles to accepting my argument will be removed.

Some of the most influential work of analytic philosophers of education has been presented as an attempt to steer a middle way between the prescriptions of child-centred theorists and more conservative approaches.[1] Because the doctrines endorsed in this book are hedged with qualifications not always found in the rhetoric of Rousseau and his successors, the reader might infer that this work embarks upon a well-travelled middle course between two equally extreme and untenable positions. This inference would be a mistake. If by a "middle course" one means an approach to problems in the philosophy of education which attests more or less equally to child-centred and opposing influences, then it is clear that such an approach is not now common, despite frequent claims to the contrary. The current dominant figures in the discipline are R.S. Peters and P.H. Hirst, and Rousseau, Dewey, and their kind have had little impact upon their thinking. In order to see this one might compare Peters's laudatory essay on Michael Oakshott, an emphatically conservative educational thinker whose influence on Peters's work is considerable, with his sharply critical articles on Rousseau and Dewey.[2] The customary strategy for Peters, Hirst, and others has been to try to how that whatever truth child-centred doctrines contain is platitudinous. Consequently they suggest that no substantial revision of established practices is needed so long as these are conducted humanely, and with a judicious regard for the child's psychological make-up. This strategy allows one to agree with much of what Rousseau and his successors have said, while at the same time the radical sting is taken out of their arguments. The idea that the curriculum should be based upon the child's interests is a case in point. Peters and Hirst would endorse this view so long as it is understood to mean that the curriculum is to be in the child's interest. That is, the curriculum should benefit the child in some way, but of course no one could sanely doubt that. They also maintain that we should try to implement the curriculum in a manner that excites the interests of students, though again one would be hard-pressed to find anyone who supposes that we should not teach in an interesting manner.[3] By subjecting each child-centred doctrine to the harsh light of conceptual analysis its appeal is supposed to disappear entirely or become something all sensible people can accept without much change to established patterns of child-rearing. This strategy is a way of debunking the child-centred tradition rather than a means of finding a *via media* between its advocates and detractors.

The route I intend to take is altogether different. I want to show that certain recognizably child-centred doctrines do have merit; and though one may have to do a bit of hedging with qualifications to see that this is the case, they are still at least quasi-radical doctrines for all that. Furthermore, talk about middle courses is extremely misleading here. It presupposes that we can interpret child-centred and opposing views along a continuum of ideas, in much the same way that we can allegedly understand political controversies in terms of a continuum which runs from the extreme left to the extreme right. The metaphor of the continuum distracts our attention from the immense internal diversity of views ordinarily classified as child-centred or conservative.

This book contains almost nothing in the way of commentary on the writings of Rousseau or his successors, apart from a substantial discussion about the deschoolers in the fourth chapter. Rousseau is an extremely elusive philosopher. The same can be said of John Dewey, who is usually, though perhaps not rightly, regarded as the major inheritor of the child-centred tradition in the twentieth century. The task of interpretation is made especially difficult by the fact that the writings of each can be construed as being in some respects at variance with the liberal thrust of child-centred education.[4] Consistency and clarity are often conspicuously absent from the pages of *Emile* and *Democracy and Education*. Because any attempt to make my own case via an interpretation of Rousseau or Dewey (or any lesser figure in the child-centred tradition) would obscure my argument beneath a thicket of scholarly exegesis, I have not chosen that course. A more significant omission in this book is the absence of any discussion about the implications of autonomy as an educational ideal for family life. I have discussed briefly this issue elsewhere,[5] but a thorough investigation here would carry us far afield. It would be necessary to elaborate and justify a detailed theory of parental rights and duties, to sort out subtle problems about the morality of state interference in family life, and to determine the proper place of educational ends in the relationship between parents and children. I have chosen to focus upon the relevance of autonomy as an educational ideal for schooling not because I think that is the more important issue but simply because it is the more manageable one. On some future occasion I hope to deal at appropriately great length with the difficulties surrounding family life which I have just mentioned.

Another aspect of this book may warrant some comment. I have already noted that the first two chapters are devoted to a discussion of the nature and value of freedom and autonomy. This portion of the book is a fairly long and involved excursion into ethics and social philosophy, only occasionally alluding to educational matters. It seemed proper to justify my views about freedom and autonomy before addressing the educational themes which concern me because any attempt to carry out both tasks *pari passu* would naturally arouse the suspicion – especially among readers averse to the child-centred tradition – that I was simply tailoring my position in ethics and social philosophy to fit the educational conclusions I wanted to reach. I hope the opening chapters show that my views about freedom and autonomy carry weight regardless of one's prior educational loyalties, and might make some readers more ready to heed the arguments of the remaining chapters than they otherwise would have been. Moreover, the opening chapters are long and involved only because they deal with matters which cannot be adequately examined with brisk simplicity. Freedom and autonomy are intellectually troublesome ideas, and no philosophical consensus has been reached about them which could support a conception of their educational relevance. For example, much of what I claim in the last three chapters about how schooling might maximize the freedom of students depends upon views about the relevance of inabilities to judgments about freedom and the connections between interests, autonomy and liberty; and because these views are very far from obviously justified, they require a rather long and intricate defence at the outset. Readers who are not interested in ethics or social philosophy per se may need some patience for these early chapters, but I hope that by the end of the book they will not feel their perseverance altogether wasted.

CHAPTER ONE

Freedom

In political and educational discourse "freedom" is a word which almost always carries a strongly positive emotional charge. Yet its descriptive content appears to vary widely from one context to another. It is a truism of intellectual history that freedom or liberty – I use the two words interchangeably – has gained the verbal allegiance of everyone; it is equally well known that this shared loyalty does not signify agreement on anything of substance. The free society of the anarchist is not at all like that of the socialist, and when one talks of the free institutions of a parliamentary democracy, those who despise the latter are apt to say that the same institutions are really instruments of oppression. In a similar way, opposing educational policies are championed under the banner of freedom. Those who espouse the ideals of a so-called liberal education have often defended their position on the basis of its putative connection with the value of liberty,[1] while their adversaries within the child-centred tradition have usually professed to be the authentic exponents of liberty in education.[2] In disputes of this kind, "freedom" has become a battleground for valuations of enormous diversity, with apparently little in the way of a range of meaning common to all combatants.

These facts make it appealing to argue that we would be better off attending to the divergent valuations underlying (and often disguised by) our common professions of concern for liberty rather than fretting about the significance of freedom per se. But that argument would be convincing only if freedom were a largely vacuous concept to be filled out according to one's own political or moral commitments. Although there is some truth to this view, it exaggerates the extent to which the meaning of freedom is contingent upon divergent value judgments. In what follows it should become clear that much of the disagreement in this area stems either from a failure to distinguish between two distinct concepts of freedom or from attempts to capture the honorific overtones of "liberty" by marking the boundaries of social or political freedom in an ideologically partisan fashion. When these two sources of controversy have been exposed, it is possible to discern a concept of freedom which has a substantial shared content, and though individuals may disagree in how the concept is applied, it is a vitally important one for all that.

The most straightforward use of the word "free" occurs when we speak of a subject which might have a certain property or exist in a certain relation but does not. This use normally carries the suggestion that it is far more desirable that the subject does not have the property or exist in the relation than that it does. For example, we speak of skies free from clouds, streets free from litter, and so on. The meaning of "freedom" here is negative in that valid application of the concept depends on the absence of something – clouds, litter, and the like. In discussing the freedom of human beings, this negative aspect is often conspicuous – we speak of freedom from hunger or oppression for example. To be free from oppression then, it might seem, is to be rid of it in much the same way as a litter-free street is rid of litter. Consequently, it might be thought that "freedom," in the sense that concerns us as moral and political beings, is identical to the concept found in these contexts. The word signifies a dyadic relation between a subject (e.g., a human being) and some condition, normally undesirable, which might apply to the subject but does not (e.g., political oppression).

However, if I speak of what I am free to do, as opposed to what I am free from, the emphasis of what I say will not be on the "negative" fact that a certain condition does not apply to me, but on the "positive" fact that a certain condition does – the fact that I am now free to do something or other, to take or relinquish a certain option. Given the marked difference in emphasis between statements about "freedom to" and "freedom from," it is easy to assume that there are two distinct concepts at work here, one positive, the other negative. Isaiah Berlin's famous essay, "Two Concepts of Liberty," appears to support this view by providing an analysis of the history of freedom as a political ideal based upon a distinction between positive and negative conceptions.[3] What I shall refer to as positive and negative freedom are not the substantive political values Berlin is mainly concerned with, but rather the ordinary ideas of "free-

dom from" and "freedom to" in which these ideologies are supposedly rooted.

Berlin points out that throughout the history of western political
thought, some writers proclaim the importance of freedom but
associate it with a society which, though self-governing, may severely circumscribe the lives of its individual members. Other political theorists who espouse the ideal of freedom have interpreted
it as requiring noninterference within a domain of private or self-
regarding conduct.[4] Since the former can be seen as being preoccupied with the value of a society's freedom to be self-determining, and the latter as championing the freedom of the individual
from the interference of others, it would seem that the values of the
former are attached to the idea of positive liberty, while those of the
latter centre upon the concept of negative liberty. The difficulty
with this position is that if one looks hard enough at any particular
instance of positive or negative liberty, it normally turns out to be
describable in terms of the other sort of liberty. One might say that
Berlin's putative adherents of positive freedom want the activity of
collective self-determination to be free from the interference of
forces outside the society and disruptive elements within it, while
adherents of negative liberty want the individual to be free to determine her life as she pleases within the area of self-regarding
conduct. Thus the dominant interest of Berlin's so-called proponents of positive freedom, given a different but perfectly accurate
description of their position, appears to be in negative freedom; and
the overriding concern of their political adversaries turns out to be
with positive freedom, given a similar descriptive change. That is
not to say that no significant difference exists between the two
schools of political thought which Berlin differentiates – there obviously is – but it is a difference to which the ordinary distinction
between positive and negative liberty is wholly irrelevant. What we
have generally in discussions about the freedom of persons is not
two distinct concepts but correlative aspects of the same concept,
one of which is brought into focus in the locution "free from ... ,"
while the other is made explicit in the locution "free to ... ." In these
contexts, freedom involves a *triadic* relation between a person, an
open option or range of options, and some constraint or range of
constraints on the exercise of choice.

Of course, not all instances of freedom include both positive and
negative aspects. Positive liberty does entail a negative dimension
because to be free to do something implies that one is free from
whatever might impede actually doing it; hence whenever the triadic relation holds, it is permissible simply to speak of positive

freedom. But negative freedom from something does not necessarily mean the positive freedom to do anything. Alfredo Rocca's defence of the fascist conception of freedom illustrates this point nicely. "Our concept of liberty is that the individual must be allowed to develop his personality in behalf of the state, for the ephemeral and infinitesimal elements of the complex and permanent life of society determine by their normal growth the development of the state. Freedom therefore is due to the citizen and to classes on condition that they exercise it in the interest of society as a whole."[5]

What Rocca regards as the legitimate exercise of freedom is more accurately described as enforced conformity to the will of those who possess power in the fascist state. If I must exercise this "freedom" in the interest of society as a whole, I do not act freely at all because I would suffer dearly if I tried to do otherwise. But there is a sense, though a trivial one, in which Rocca is an advocate of freedom, and it is this which gives his argument some semblance of sense. What he is saying, to put it in plain English, is that the full development of the state according to the public interest requires that we free ourselves *from* all obstacles to that goal, including the morally paltry predilections of mere individuals; but since these same individuals are also "elements" of the state, they too are freed from certain constraints in this process. What Rocca is really after might be described as purely negative freedom: obstacles to a certain state of affairs are removed but no net increase in the range of our open options is thereby obtained.

Although the concept of purely negative freedom can be found in more morally respectable contexts than fascist bombast, it is still a concept of negligible interest. When human beings regard something as desirable – and this will commonly have nothing to do with positive liberty – they will regard the removal of obstacles to its attainment as desirable. It is in this empty sense that we are all "for" freedom, or more precisely, the removal of whatever obstacles impede us in seeking whatever we desire. To ask about the value of removing obstacles apart from our goals, as if that might be valuable in itself, is absurd. (It is rather like asking about the value of absence, regardless of what is absent.) Moreover, the use of this concept in describing or recommending particular policies, without a clear understanding of how it differs from positive liberty, has the unfortunate consequence of suggesting that in every case freedom is at stake in some significant respect. Consider the following statement of John Dewey: "The only freedom that is of enduring importance is freedom of intelligence, that is to say, freedom of observation and judgment on behalf of purposes that are intrinsically worthwhile."[6] It is certainly true that greater intelligence might enlarge the range of one's positive freedom in many circumstances, but it does not follow that the removal of any and every obstacle to greater intelligence will have that effect. Perhaps compulsory schooling until the age of fifty would greatly improve our "observation and judgment on behalf of purposes that are intrinsically worthwhile," but the fact that it did would not entail that we thereby would enjoy a greater range of positive freedom. If the removal of obstacles to greater intelligence is the *only* freedom that matters, as Dewey argues, then freedom does not matter in any interesting sense at all – it is greater intelligence that counts for everything, and he merely confuses the issue by stressing the relevance of freedom in this connection.

The philosophically important sense of "freedom," is positive liberty with its triadic relation.[7] A thorough analysis of this concept would require a detailed examination of each of the variables in the relation. It would be necessary to look at the concept of a person in order to clarify who can count as a subject of freedom, and then we would face the problem of explaining what makes something an option or object of choice. I shall not address any of the thorny philosophical questions about persons and choices here because it is unnecessary. Nothing I wish to defend in this book presupposes any really controversial answer to those questions, at least as far as I am aware. But the way in which I conceive the second variable in the triadic relation – what one can be free from – is more than a bit contentious. A long-standing tradition in Anglo-American philosophy counts only a certain narrowly limited range of constraints as impediments to freedom, and this tradition has certainly had an impact upon nonphilosophical discourse. The tradition is far from salutary and since the way in which I believe it should be revised is central to the arguments of chapters three and four, it is important to dwell on its deficiencies.

It is widely thought that because only external interference, or certain specified kinds of external interference, can curtail freedom, no other constraints are relevant to the estimation of freedom.[8] I shall call this "the traditional criterion of relevant constraint." (The appellation is a bit misleading since it really designates a family of possible criteria rather than a single criterion. Philosophers can and do take a large variety of possible positions under the traditional rubric as I have defined it. It is nonetheless convenient to bundle these positions together because my criticisms will apply regardless of variations within the family of criteria.)

Physical restraint and external compulsion are the paradigms of relevant constraint for proponents of this view. The mere absence of an external advantage, such as wealth, has nothing to do with judgments about freedom, and internal disadvantages are also beside the point. As Herbert Spencer noted, impoverished parents who could not afford to educate their children prior to the introduction of free schooling were nonetheless free to do so.[9] It was only poverty which prevented them from sending their children to school and poverty does not limit freedom. Similarly, a dyslexic adult does not suffer any loss of freedom because of her dyslexia since mental disabilities are irrelevant constraints.

If we were to accept the traditional criterion of constraint, rather stringent requirements would be imposed upon how we deploy the concept of freedom. One could not say, for example, that compulsory schooling can enhance the liberty of its clients by removing various intellectual incapacities which prevent them from availing themselves of a wide variety of important options. And by affecting how we conceive freedom, the traditional criterion will influence which policies we select or reject in order to express our allegiance to freedom as a social ideal. Suppose we assume that liberty is of supreme importance in matters of social policy and at the same time accept the traditional criterion of constraint. Compulsory schooling then would be unacceptable. We could not even argue for state-funded voluntary schooling since the taxation necessary to sustain it would be an extensive infringement upon liberty. If one believes there are morally important things other than freedom, then this line of reasoning will not necessarily be convincing since compulsion will sometimes be justified in terms of the values with which freedom competes. Nevertheless, many persons would still want to say that a loss of freedom is a notable, albeit sometimes necessary evil; and therefore, given the traditional criterion, the libertarian argument against compulsory or state-funded schooling should have considerable *prima facie* appeal for them. As a matter of empirical fact, the libertarian argument against compulsory or state-funded schooling is not often taken seriously. However that merely attests to our tendency to forget what we profess to believe about the value of freedom when issues concerning childhood and education arise.

Why should we accept the traditional criterion? One answer is that any alternative would distort what is normally and hence properly meant when liberty figures in practical discourse.[10] Fidelity to ordinary language is not the all-encompassing philosophical virtue it was once thought to be, but we certainly should be wary of altering our established moral vocabulary in ways that might impoverish it. Nevertheless, the answer is still patently unconvincing because departures from the traditional criterion are not even faintly eccentric. If I said that I was not free to meet you for lunch because of a promise I had already made, my statement would not be unintelligible or odd, but it would imply that promises can curb one's freedom. Since promises cannot be interpreted as any kind of external interference, the traditional criterion and ordinary language part company at this point. Further, the sort of examples used to support or illustrate the traditional criterion can be more plausibly interpreted in a manner which consorts with a much broader view of relevant constraint. Spencer's remark about the freedom of the poor before the institution of mass schooling would be unobjectionable if it were understood as an elliptical statement about what the poor were *legally* free to do before that institution was created. Construed as an assertion about what they were free to do without any such qualification, the statement is false since poverty is commonly recognized as a relevant constraint. A woman who has fallen on hard economic times might complain of the loss of freedom as a result of poverty without straining our sense of linguistic propriety. We can also agree that dyslexia, like other handicaps, does not impair one's liberty in certain respects. Because a dyslexic adult may enjoy the same legal rights and be subject to the same legal obligations as others, there are contexts in which we could truly say that dyslexia does not impair freedom, once it is tacitly understood that legal entitlements and constraints are the exclusive concern. But it hardly makes sense to say that the dyslexic enjoys the same freedom as others when it comes to choosing a career.

In ordinary language , a much less strict view is often taken of how freedom can be impaired than some defenders of the traditional criterion would acknowledge, though others are sometimes ready to recognize this fact. These others maintain that they are interested in social or political liberty, which has to be distinguished from other forms of freedom, and it is the traditional criterion which enables them to distinguish the concept they favour.[11] But once this move is made, the defence of the traditional criterion in terms of ordinary language is tacitly relinquished. For if there were more than one triadic concept of freedom discoverable in our established ways of speaking, one which conformed to the traditional criterion while the others did not, then whatever presumption there is in favour of ordinary language could not tell us which concept applies when we raise the question of the value of freedom in social or educational philosophy. Pre-empting the titles "social freedom" or "political liberty" for the concept one favours merely begs the question.

Attention to the diversity of ways in which the language of freedom is employed shows that we do not consistently adhere to *any* specific criterion of relevant constraint. There are times when moral obligations are virtually all we take into account, as when someone contemplating civil disobedience asks her conscience if she is really free to flout the authority of the state. In some situations physical restraint is the exclusive concern. When hardened criminals are released from prison one might ruefully note that they are free to resume their illegal activities, though in other contexts we will recognize that legal prohibitions curtail freedom just as surely as physical confinement. There are also occasions where emotional states are assumed to be a relevant constraint and others where they are not. "I am not free to marry you because I love someone else" makes perfect sense under conceivable circumstances, but we usually do not consider love as a constraint upon choice.

Assumptions about what constraints are relevant alter in everyday language according to differences in our purposes from one context to another. This might make it appear that there is no genuine philosophical problem here. The expertise of the philosopher is not sufficient to show which purposes are apropriate, and it can hardly be maintained that extensive variation in what we take to be a relevant constraint is in itself deplorable. Nevertheless, what might be established is that serious reflection on fundamental political or educational matters is better served by one criterion of relevance rather than others; and that conclusion might hold whatever particular purposes reasonable persons may bring to such reflection. Arguments designed to support the conclusion for some criterion are simply attempts to fix the boundaries of those freedoms of ethical concern within the shifting territory of positive liberty. This subset of positive liberty will preoccupy the remainder of the book, and "freedom" and "liberty" should be understood as abbreviated references to it.

A familiar argument can be adduced at this point to support the traditional criterion. It has been asserted that if we adopt a lax view of constraint so that ignorance, coercion, poverty, and so on are all treated as germane, we will conflate values which should be carefully distinguished. At least part of the point of analysis of notions which have political or educational significance is to provide a conceptual framework within which the problems of policy-making can be clearly and profitably posed – a criterion of relevant constraint which blurs important distinctions is obviously to be rejected. The supposed theoretical advantage of the traditional criterion is that it forestalls the softening of boundaries between freedom and such competing values as wealth and education. Berlin has made this point:

Useless freedoms should be made usable, but they are not identical with the conditions indispensable for their utility. This is not a merely pedantic distinction, for if it is ignored, the meaning and value of freedom of choice is apt to be downgraded. In their zeal to create social and economic conditions in which alone freedom is of genuine value, men tend to forget freedom itself; and if it is remembered it is likely to be pushed aside to make room for those other values with which the reformers or revolutionaries have become preoccupied.[12]

Presumably, Berlin means something like this. Those who oppose the traditional criterion of constraint are inclined to ignore the fact that state interference necessarily limits liberty, and where this fact is acknowledged, they are apt to discount its importance. Preoccupied with the laudable purposes an enlarged state may prosecute, they naturally tend to overlook the costs to freedom which their policies exact. Therefore Berlin would seem to argue, we should opt for the traditional criterion of constraint in order to guard against the unfortunate psychological tendency to forget freedom with which alternative views are associated.

It should be stressed that this is not to suggest that these alternative views imply that we should disregard the liberties curtailed by state interference. The more plausible alternatives certainly carry no such implications. For that reason Berlin has to take the weak position that the alternatives to the traditional theory are associated, as a matter of empirical fact, with the neglect of liberty. He gives no evidence to show that this is a matter of empirical fact, as opposed to mere speculation on his part, and even if he did, it could hardly justify the conclusion he wants to reach. If those who adhere to a certain criterion of relevant constraint are apt to make objectionable judgments about freedom wholly unwarranted by their criterion, this surely would not give them enough reason to abandon it. They would certainly have reason to be vigilant against those errors they are prone to make, but that is another matter.

Berlin introduces an important distinction between freedom and the conditions under which freedom becomes usable in the passage examined above. If we probe this distinction, we will quickly realize just what is wrong with the traditional criterion. He maintains that there are many things we are free to do which we are also unable to do because of poverty, ignorance, poor health, and so forth; and where there is freedom without the ability to take advantage of it, the freedom is unusable. A usable liberty is thus a liberty to do something which one can effectively choose to do (or not do). Berlin maintains that unusable liberties are worthless, though he does not explain why this is so.

Suppose I am one of those impoverished nineteenth-century parents whom Spencer believed were free but unable to send their children to school. (I shall describe my situation in a manner that conforms to the traditional criterion). There is no benefit I have which I would be deprived of if my unusable liberty were taken away because there is nothing of value I can do or enjoy by virtue of that liberty. To be sure, I am likely to prefer being free and unable rather than unfree and unable. If I had previously been legally prohibited from educating my children and the prohibition were abolished, my liberty might hearten me as a step in the right direction. But if someone convinced me that my poverty would always prevent me from using that liberty, I would have to conclude that my new entitlement was no real advantage at all. As long as they are unusable, liberties are worthless. Moreover, social deprivations make them unusable. Insofar as freedom concerns policy making, it has to be usable freedom.

Berlin and others who share his idea of liberty claim that they wish to clarify the status of freedom as a distinct source of value in matters of policy, but their conception of relevant constraint does not serve that purpose. Where the fact that valuable liberties have to be usable is appreciated – and it is by no means always appreciated by exponents of the traditional criterion[13] – we find a bizarre and misleading view of the relationship between freedom and its value. The only way of increasing freedom, according to these philosophers, is by minimizing external interference; but to realize freedom as a value it has to be made usable, and this very often necessitates greater external interference, such as heavier taxation to fund welfare programmes. Therefore, the more freedom we have, the less value it may tend to have for the disadvantaged. Our desire to safeguard liberty and our desire to ensure its worth for all will often lead to incompatible policies.

The traditional criterion muddles the relationship between liberty and its value. The importance of keeping that relationship in focus can justify extending the notion of relevant constraint to include all inabilities other than those which have some logical impossibility as their object. All inabilities which met this condition would be considered as restrictions upon the subject's range of open options ("usable liberty," in Berlin's terms) – restrictions which we should perhaps strive to eradicate. In other words, any such inability is conceivably an evil, *qua* an impediment to choice, that is relevant to our practical deliberations. The importance of this point becomes obvious if one bears in mind that an incurable disease, for instance, may deprive me of my most cherished options just as thoroughly as acts of coercion. In the former case, we are certainly more likely to regard the loss as a purely natural misfortune rather than a matter of moral significance, but that view is not necessarily justified. Suppose there are reasons to believe that a cure for my disease could be found if only public resources were deflected from certain wasteful projects into medical research and alternative uses for these resources were not clearly of greater moment than finding a cure. In that case, my misfortune looks more like an injustice than a merely natural occurrence. The obvious danger of drawing the boundaries of relevant constraint more narrowly, so that incurable diseases, ignorance, and similar disabling conditions do not count, is that our perception of wrongs resulting from their presence becomes obscured. We will say that whoever has these inabilities endures no loss of freedom, and *a fortiori* no loss of freedom to which they are morally entitled. This slurs over the crucial fact that inability restricts effective choice, which the value of freedom presupposes, just as surely as any act of external interference. In claiming that this is a fact, I am not assuming some contestable theory about the value of freedom. I merely assume, what is hardly contestable, that insofar as the freedom to do certain things is a matter of interest, these must be things we can effectively choose to do, and the criterion of relevant constraint we adopt in moral theory should reflect that necessity.

A sufficient condition of being unfree to do something is that one is unable to do it. That is the essence of the preceding discussion. It is worth noting that by accepting this conclusion one does not obliterate the intuitively important distinction between being able to do something and being free to do it. Consider again some of the implications of Alfredo Rocca's fascist conception of liberty. Rocca maintains that "freedom" is due to any citizen only when it is exercised in the interests of the fascist state. Presumably, the authorities would have to ensure that citizens were able to act in this fashion. For example, it would be necessary to keep them informed about what kind of conduct is supposed to advance the cause of fascism. But being able to act would not necessarily mean they were free.

Liberties are open options, and the openness of an option is determined by the absence of relevant constraints to taking *and* foregoing it. If I am able to act in the interests of the fascist state, but unable to do otherwise without incurring the wrath of the authorities, then I am in no position to act freely. Joel Feinberg has come near the truth on this point.

I have an open option with respect to a given act X when I am permitted to do X and I am also permitted to do *not-X* (that is to omit doing X) so that it is up to me entirely whether I do X or not. If I am permitted to do X but not permitted to do *not-X* , I am not in any usual sense at liberty to do X, for if X is the only thing I am permitted to do, it follows that I am compelled to do X, and compulsion, of course, is the plain opposite of liberty. The possession of a liberty is simply the possession of alternative possibilities of action ...[14]

The only thing amiss here is the assumption that compulsion alone can deprive us of liberty. In fact, Feinberg could have avoided that mistake by attending more carefully to the implications of his own, very useful definition of a liberty, for it is obvious that we can be deprived of "alternative possibilities of action" by means other than compulsion.

A final complication remains in the analysis of freedom which I should note in passing. When we make comparisons about the extent of freedom possessed by citizens in different societies, or estimate the overall scope of someone's liberty, we are necessarily quantifying ranges of open options. It does not seem possible to do this without bringing other values into play and that is the germ of truth in the charge that freedom is an almost vacuous concept which each of us may stretch to fit our own particular preferences. In deciding whether of not Joan has more overall freedom than Jane, we do not simply count open options in an evaluatively neutral way. We assume that the absence of relevant constraint in some areas of choice is more important than its absence in others. Freedom in decisions about religious affiliation adds more to our overall liberty than freedom in decisions about which flavour of ice-cream to select, or so we ordinarily think. This problem is dealt with in more depth in the final section of chapter two because my views about it depend upon the connection between freedom and autonomy, which will be explained there.

In many instances freedom is prized not for what it is (or not only for what it is), but for what it causes. By ensuring that freedom prevails we help to bring about some valuable end other than freedom, such as greater happiness, and because the end is valuable, so too are the means by which it is achieved. In cases where freedom is valuable for its causal effects, it has instrumental value.

It would be absurd to maintain that freedom does not often have instrumental value in the world as we know it, but by itself that fact can only provide a rather fragile defence of its importance in matters of policy. If freedom is just an instrumental value, then we can permissibly dispense with it whenever some net good, no matter how slight in itself, would follow from constraint. Moreover, we should take no account of freedom itself in the weighing of goods and evils. Ambitious arguments regarding liberty as an instrumental value have often been offered, but they achieve rather less than their adherents would like to think.

In *On Liberty*, J.S. Mill asserted that freedom of thought and action, at least where harm to others is not at stake, has immediate social consequences which in turn conduce to greater happiness. He claimed that freedom enables us to choose the best theories as well as the best forms of life, and it ensures that we maintain a vigorous rather than a merely nominal adherence to what we choose.[15] Mill's enthusiasm for liberty, however, outstrips his capacity to justify it as a means to happiness.

First, though there are specific liberties which undoubtedly contribute to intellectual progress, there is just as surely a host of constraints which serves the same function. The conditions of successful inquiry can no more provide an argument for freedom *simpliciter* in thought and speech than they can yield a defence of constraint *simpliciter*. Progress in science, say, does not occur through a "free for all" in which ignorant novices can pursue or promulgate their theories as freely as accomplished scholars. Inquiry should certainly be conducted in a manner receptive to possible contributions from the iconoclastic outsider, but even this voice would surely be drowned in the cacophony that would ensue from indiscriminate access to research facilities or freedom for everyone to publish in learned journals.

It is also far from certain that greater happiness will inevitably follow if we strive to enhance freedom in the selection of forms of life. We would have more room for the exercise of autonomy and individuality, and perhaps this would make many of us happier. But there might well be disadvantages to the "open society" espoused by Mill which could make it undesirable, all things considered, for anyone exclusively concerned with maximizing happiness.

New liberties might create new anxieties for many persons who would be happier if they could avoid the burdens of choice. Being free to choose from among an extensive range of forms of life might often result in intense frustration if what is chosen turns out to be badly suited to one's talents or temperament. One could not be consoled by the thought that others were responsible for one's mal-adjustment. Vinit Haksar has recently shown that there are many possible features of the "closed society" despised by liberals which one would have to find attractive if one prized freedom merely instrumentally, as Mill professed to do.[16] I do not want to suggest that an exclusively instrumental approach to this matter will oblige one to oppose liberty as vehemently as Mill supported it. The point is rather that Mill's argument depends on some clearly false premises (those pertaining to freedom in inquiry) and other highly speculative premises (those relating to freedom in the selection and pursuit of forms of life). So if one shares Mill's view that freedom is just a means to happiness, one must also admit that it is a much less clearly reliable and potent means than he supposed it to be.

These limitations of Mill's defence of freedom are typical of arguments for liberty which rely exclusively on instrumental considerations, regardless of whether or not happiness is taken to be the ultimate good. If I give someone the freedom to do X, I must also leave her at liberty to do not-X because freedom implies that it is the responsibility of the agent to decide if she will do what she is free to do. Whether or not her freedom conduces to some desirable end will almost certainly depend upon what particular choices she makes. Choosing X will make one more wise or happy, say, but choosing not-X will have the opposite effect. The problem this creates is not just that the freedom to do not-X means that the instrumental value cannot be guaranteed in advance. More important, our knowledge is frequently such that we cannot be even moderately confident that the right choices will be made. Therefore, in such cases we cannot be even moderately confident that freedom will have instrumental value. Our knowledge of others is not so exact that we can easily predict their choices, though we know enough to be sure that their choices will often fail to maximize desirable consequences.

A purely instrumental theory of the value of freedom leads to a liberalism which is at best anaemic and hesitant – a conclusion with which many of us will feel uncomfortable. For instance, one of the most renowned contemporary liberals, Ronald Dworkin, maintains that certain liberties, such as freedom of speech, are so precious that only a catastrophe or something very near it could warrant their sacrifice.[17] I suspect that many would find Dworkin's position intuitively appealing, but nothing like his tenacious respect for liberty can be justified in instrumental terms.

The most obvious alternative is to argue that liberty is not only (sometimes) an instrumental value; it is also an intrinsic value, something we rightly prize for its own sake. That is to say, there is a value which all liberties have irrespective of any other facts about them, a value they bear just because they are liberties. By regarding freedom in this way, one is led to the belief that there is always at least a presumption in favour of freedom (presumptive principle). Whenever we settle for less than we might, there must be a reason sufficiently weighty to warrant our acceptance of less than maximum freedom. Yet the presumptive principle only makes sense as an affirmation of the intrinsic value of freedom if we have a method of determining what counts as an overall loss or gain in liberty from one situation to another *without* bringing other values into play. If there were no such method (and I think there is none), then the presumptive principle would be tied to those other values which are tacitly invoked when we try to calculate overall losses or gains; hence the principle would entail that freedom is not valuable for its own sake but only by virtue of its relation to those other values. But let us assume for the moment that we have such a method so that the presumptive principle can be understood as affirming the intrinsic value of freedom. (It is worthwhile to entertain this possibility since my claim that we lack the relevant method is by no means a philosophical commonplace.[18])

Unfortunately, based on that interpretation, the presumptive principle could not help us evade the implausible implications of a purely instrumental theory of the value of freedom. It is crucial to bear in mind that whatever the intrinsic value of freedom, it is to be found equally in all freedoms since it logically cannot vary according to different facts about this or that specific open option. The liberty to smash storefront windows and form monopolies cannot differ, with respect to its intrinsic value, from the liberty to proclaim one's religious convictions, because each is equally liberty, and that is the only relevant fact if we are just considering their intrinsic value.[19] Of course, to prize all freedoms equally as freedoms is not necessarily to value them equally, all things considered. Although the freedom to do X and to do Y may have the same intrinsic value, the fact that one militates against the realization of some other value while the other does not leads, other things being equal, to different overall evaluations of them. Therefore, the claim that freedom has intrinsic value can be reconciled with the belief that some freedoms require special protection while others should be sacrificed.

But this conclusion is still unsatisfactory. We were led to consider the possibility that freedom is an intrinsic value by realizing that attempts to establish its importance solely on instrumental grounds fail to support fairly widely held beliefs about the immense significance of certain liberties, such as freedom of speech or religion. A purely instrumental theory is thus counterintuitive for many persons, and though that is no reason to reject the theory, it is certainly a reason to look for principles which might support the intuitions the theory cannot sustain. But these intuitions cannot be sustained by arguments derived from the putative fact that freedom has intrinsic value. Because arguments of that sort support all freedoms equally, they cannot tell us why some are precious and others are not.

At this point one might conclude that the counterintuitive implications of the purely instrumental theory just have to be accepted. But that is too hasty because it presupposes that only instrumental and intrinsic values exist. Something may be valuable not for its own sake nor for the sake of what it causes but because it is partly constitutive of a larger complex which is valuable for its own sake. I shall call this a constitutive value. An example will help explain this. Suppose Mary discovered a new and very beautiful sonnet by Shakespeare but revealed her discovery to the world only after erasing the couplet. Now the harm she did is not to be explained just by saying that the couplet had intrinsic aesthetic value. Indeed, the couplet might not even make any sense apart from its context within the poem. It would also be wrong to suggest that in erasing the couplet she destroyed something which was valuable as a means to the intrinsic aesthetic value of the complete sonnet. The constitutive elements of a work of art are not related to the completed product as means to an end for the simple reason that they make up "the end" – their value is properly regarded as constitutive rather than instrumental. Mary's sin was to destroy a very weighty constitutive value in that the removal of the couplet seriously detracted from the intrinsic value of the entire poem.

I want to argue that autonomy is an intrinsic good (and also an important constitutive one) and that freedom has constitutive value because it bears a certain connection to the ideal of personal autonomy or self-rule.[20] I also want to argue that some liberties have extremely weighty constitutive value because they have an especially intimate connection with the good of autonomy. What I have in mind is this. The possession of freedom is not strictly a constituent of the autonomous character. My character might instantiate autonomy more fully than anyone who has ever lived. Yet that possibility is also compatible with my languishing in a dungeon somewhere, unable to stir without the permission of my gaolers. Nonetheless, freedom is a constituent of a life in which autonomy can *flourish* because autonomy cannot be exercised in the absence of freedom. I assume that if we value a certain ideal of character, we must prize not only its possession but also what constitutes its flourishing in particular lives. Therefore, by valuing self-rule we are committed to valuing freedom. I hope to show that this commitment supports the distinction we make between the intuitively important and other liberties.

If I can defend this line of reasoning, we would have a more secure and intuitively appealing conception of the value of freedom than purely instrumental considerations can provide. But even before I can sketch that conception, a much clearer understanding of the nature of personal autonomy is necessary.

CHAPTER TWO

Autonomy

A superficial familiarity with contemporary ethics or political or educational theory will reveal just how prominent autonomy is as an ideal of human character. It forms parts of a configuration of ideas each of which has enormous importance for us: freedom, individuality, and respect. We often think of autonomy as a characteristic of persons essential to the maintenance of a free society. It also seems to be a prerequisite of individuality as that is ordinarily conceived. Certain forms of morally degrading conduct express a lack of respect for other persons in part because they seriously impede the individual in the exercise of autonomy or in transcending the limitations of a life in which autonomy is barely realized. For example, indoctrination may be denounced on these grounds. As I have described them here these conceptual connections between autonomy and other liberal values are still very hazy. One use of an analysis of autonomy, and one test of its adequacy, is that it should help us to begin elaborating them in a precise and plausible way.

The word "autonomy" does not exhibit a highly stable pattern of use in either theoretical or ordinary discourse which we could simply describe, and then approve for philosophical purposes, with minor alterations at most. But neither does it provide us with a conceptual *tabula rasa* upon which we can inscribe whatever sense we choose. Clearly, it is an idea not without substance but still rather inchoate.[1] The relation of autonomy to freedom might be described in its broad outlines by a fairly sophisticated user of the language; but to discuss that relation in any detail obliges one partly to create its meaning. Success in this creative endeavour will ultimately be determined by whether the analysis proves to be a useful tool in dealing with the substantive problems pertaining to the rather fluid concept or family of concepts which we currently share. The central problem is this: can autonomy be elucidated as an ideal of character which bears a high degree of value? If so, does that ideal yield a powerful argument for prizing freedom?

Personal autonomy essentially pertains to the regulation of the will. It applies to the way we form our beliefs because that is an activity of mind amenable to the will. (I shall defend this odd-sounding claim below.) The regulation of the will occurs partly in the control one exercises over that set of propensities which gives general shape to the individual self and the course of her life. I shall refer to this bundle of propensities as one's motivational structure.[2] The regulation of the will is also evident in the way these propensities are brought to bear in choosing this specific option rather than that one. Of course, there is a subtle interplay between these dual aspects to the control of the will: the propensities we cultivate not only incline us towards specific options but, as Aristotle pointed out,[3] it is through the disciplined choosing of certain things rather than others that we strengthen some propensities and weaken or preclude the development of others. I shall argue that strongly autonomous persons are distinguished from others because they display a high degree of realism and independence of mind in the way they regulate their wills. Any behaviour which can be explained in terms of the agent's choices will manifest these characteristics at least minimally, although my concern will be with autonomy as an ideal which is only faintly reflected in many lives.

Before explaining what I mean by " realism" and "independence of mind," I shall discuss the concept of interest in some detail. The individual's interests constitute the very core of her motivational structure. A study of that concept will help us to understand how the will can be regulated in an autonomous fashion.

The meaning of "interest" I want to deal with is not the one employed when we speak of what is in the interest of so and so. What is in my interest is whatever, roughly speaking, is to my personal advantage. This normative idea is to be contrasted with a range of uses of "interest" which are purely descriptive in character. If I say that I am interested in X, I am, in part, classifying certain feelings I am inclined to have. These feelings may or may not be personally advantageous. I shall argue that to have an interest, in this sense, involves making a certain sort of value judgment. But in professing an interest, one is, nonetheless, simply saying something about her own activity of mind. Given that I am not deceived as to my own mental states, I cannot be mistaken as to what I am interested in. Given the same self-knowledge, I can still be very much mistaken as to what is in my interest.

What does it mean to feel interested in something? Quite obviously, it entails desiring to give something or other one's attention and effort in certain ways. The necessity of this particular desire is part of what distinguishes feelings of interest from mere likings, and the contrast between these concepts discloses something important about how feelings of interest are bound up with our judgments about what matters in life. I may like someone while being consistently bored in her presence. I might regard her as a fine person without feeling in the least inclined to think about her or to seek out her company. Likings can be sustained when their object is persistently taken for granted or ignored. The same is not true of interests. Admittedly, the expression of a liking *may* involve effort and attention, but the nature of the mental engagement must be more shallow than in the case of interest. If I say "I rather like Shelley's poetry but it has never really interested me" (i.e., provoked feelings of interest) the intelligibility of my statement clearly depends on a distinction in the degree to which an object might evoke one's energies and emotions. Evidently, Shelley is the sort of poet I might read to while away an hour, but he is not one I have ever felt like studying intently. Likings are less important in a person's life, at least from her own perspective, than interests because they do not involve the same depth of mental engagement. That is why it makes no sense to say that raptures of wonder and joy attend doing what one merely likes to do. These emotions presuppose a kind of evaluation inconsistent with mere liking.

To feel interested, an individual has to be at least inclined to make a certain positive value judgment about the object of that feeling. A difference exists – a subtle but important one – between saying that I feel tempted to hurt someone and saying that I feel interested in doing so. In both cases I indicate that I am attracted to a certain course of action, but "tempted" and "interested" imply different evaluations of the object of attraction. "Tempted" clearly expresses disapproval of the intended action: what we conceive to be good inspires but it does not tempt. On the other hand, the evaluation implied by "interested" is doubtless weaker, but there is surely an implicit admission that I am inclined to commend the course of action I contemplate. Married persons who feel interested in having an affair are not simply attracted by the prospect of extra-marital sex. Their belief in monogamy must also be a bit shaky, at least when their feelings are occurrent.

So far I have been talking about interests as occurrent feelings, but we can also use the same word to refer to propensities which are not entirely reducible to such feelings. My feeling of interest as I listen to the music of Bach on the radio is no isolated episode. Its significance only becomes apparent as part of a much larger pattern of mentation. Similar experiences evoked by the same composer's music have been a recurrent part of my life for quite some time, and have motivated repeated actions, such as buying records and attending concerts. It is partly because of this enduring feature of my life, and my expectation that it will continue, that I can claim to be interested in Bach's music, even when I do not currently feel interested in it. This is a sense of "being interested" which requires a certain coherent pattern of mental activity, composed of intermittent feelings of interest and inclinations to act in ways which sustain these feelings. Yet this sense of "being interested" also requires something else.

Suppose Carol is a scientist who has been passionately absorbed in a particular line of research. She becomes convinced that despite its intrinsic fascination, she must quit the research because her discoveries will be used for evil purposes. She informs her patrons that she is no longer interested in the work they have funded and turns her attention to other matters. Nevertheless, from time to time she might feel that she had made a mistake. The intrinsic appeal of her abandoned inquiries is revived in the mind, and on those occasions she is somewhat inclined to think that she was a bit too moralistic in her decision to abandon them. She is still prone to feel interested in the questions which once inspired her research; and she is still liable to act in ways likely to induce these feelings, by poring over old laboratory notes and the like. Now despite these inclinations, could Carol not sincerely say that such questions no longer figure among her interests? For although she is prone to feel interested in her previous research, her considered judgment, which invariably prevails against these feelings, is that her previous research is a mere source of temptation. I have already shown that feelings of interest imply that one is at least inclined to make a certain value judgment about the object of one's feelings. Now it would appear that interest as a propensity entails a rather fuller commitment to a judgment of this sort. Carol does not *believe* that her previous research is still a worthy enterprise, notwithstanding intermittent doubts on that point. Therefore, she can truly say that it is no longer one of her interests.

This example brings into relief the fact that interests (in one sense) entail beliefs of a certain kind. Carol's situation makes it plain that these beliefs reflect what Charles Taylor has called "strong evaluation." Taylor points out that persons do not, at least characteristically, evaluate alternatives just in terms of the sheer pull of each option upon their desires. The strong evaluator assumes that "some desires or desired consummations can be judged as bad, base, ignoble, trivial, superficial, unworthy and so on,"[4] and the judgments she makes according to these criteria will profoundly affect whichever desires eventually prevail in her conduct. For Carol, the desire to pursue research which has morally damaging consequences cannot pass the test of strong evaluation. As a result, what otherwise might have continued to be a consuming personal interest becomes just a nagging source of temptation. It is not that she subscribes to criteria of strong evaluation extrinsic to her interests. Rather, her interest in living a morally decent life occupies a deeper position in her scheme of values than her commitment to untrammelled inquiry. Hence inquiry must give way when it clashes with her moral loyalties.

There is a final aspect to the connection between interest and evaluation which deserves our attention. Its relevance becomes apparent if we slightly alter the details of Carol's story. Suppose Carol's passionate absorption in her investigations was wholly due to voracious careerism. Her research was just a route to money and status, and in her candid moments she would admit that in itself it was trivial and boring. In that event, by abandoning her work in an act of strong evaluation, she would not, by the same token, be renouncing an interest in her work simply because there would be no interest to renounce. In this altered version of the story, Carol is no more interested in her own research than a child who works intently on a tedious science project only to avoid the wrath of a parent or teacher. Of course, Carol does believe that her work is valuable – as an effective means of becoming rich and famous – but the *reasons* which support the belief are not the kind which are relevant to having an interest. One does not really have an interest in science per se unless one ascribes intrinsic value to experiences and achievements internal to scientific inquiry. The same point applies, *mutatis mutandis*, to other interests.[5] The things we value instrumentally may be things we ardently desire, but they do not necessarily inspire even the faintest spark of interest.

I have dwelt at length on the relation between interest and evaluation because it reveals why one's interests are central to one's sense of self. This goes a long way towards explaining why the ongoing shaping of one's interests might be essential to self-rule. Consider Dewey's strange claim that we identify with the things we are interested in. A.R. White has argued that this is sheer drivel if we take it literally.[6] If I am interested in the music of Bach, I do not thereby *become* the music of Bach. But a literal reading is hardly suitable here. Dewey probably meant that our interests are definitive of who we are in that the meaning of our lives largely depends upon them. Imagine what it would be like to lose all your interests. You would no longer be the same person, except in superficial respects, because your interests give your life a sense of significant continuity. A life without interests would be a life felt to be virtually meaningless. Certainly there would be no room for strong evaluation, and things could be intrinsically valued only in the most attenuated sense. In such circumstances, it is logically possible to like certain things, and experience the pleasures that ensue when one has what one likes. But having whatever one likes is at best a very small comfort when one is interested in nothing.

The shaping of a human being's interests and the way this determines decisions, and hence conduct, in interaction with other propensities are mental processes subject to reason. This brings us to the first condition of autonomy. The strongly autonomous self is to be distinguished from others partly by a level of rationality at which the motivational structure is developed in a realistic fashion and occurrent desires are regulated in the same manner. Realism is a matter of controlling the self in that "spirit of truthfulness" which Raimond Gaita takes to be the essence of integrity.[7] This notion of realism is obscure as it stands, but properly elucidated captures the contrast between reason as it functions in the life where autonomy is instantiated to a high degree and the life in which it is only faintly shown.

Before proceeding further I want to prevent one possible misunderstanding. As I interpret it, "realism" signifies a certain ideal of rationality or reasonableness. For the reader acquainted with some of the current literature on the subject of autonomy, this claim may invoke associations I do not want to build into the concept. Much of this literature connects autonomy with reason in a way that gives great emphasis to criticism and ratiocination.[8] The autonomous life is supposed to be the meticulously examined life; it is one that revolves around the giving and seeking of reasons. I choose the word "realism," however, to designate a persistent orientation of the mind towards reality and a corresponding suppression of the various ways human beings are apt to evade reality. This orientation can and does manifest itself strongly in lives where the giving and seeking of reasons is not a central preoccupation. In confronting the reality of one's nature and circumstances, it may become clear that the best possible life is one that affords a latitude for spontaneity and unreflective absorption in certain activities which severely curbs the practice of criticism. Indeed, in some situations a greater facility in the giving and seeking of reasons may impede rather than enhance realism. For example, my skill in moral argument may make me more resourceful in self-deception about my moral failures.

In "tradition-directed" cultures, as David Riesman has called them, the extent to which the meaning of life depends upon one's own choice is meagre because tradition so often precludes choice.[9] The interests which befit specific roles are norrowly demarcated, and roles are allocated according to customs which leave little space for individual predilections. One is born to be a warrior, a hunter, and so forth. Such cultures are rapidly fading and our distance from them is partly evidenced by the assumption we are apt to make that the meaning of one's life is something one creates in large part (or fails to create) rather than something that is just found in immemorial and unchangeable traditions. But if our interests were bound up with the meaning of our lives in the manner I suggested above, it might seem wrong to suggest that there could be much room in any circumstances for *creating* their meaning. Talk of creation carries implications of responsibility for what is created. It is far from clear, however, that there is any room for personal responsibility in this context. One cannot, by a fiat of the will, acquire or extinguish an interest any more than one can decrease one's height by the same means. There is an absurdity in the behavior of a teacher who commands her pupils to be interested in Shakespeare which she does not evince when she merely orders them to pay attention. Commands only make sense when what is commanded can be brought about by a direct act of will. Interest is just not like that. Therefore, the formation of a person's interests may seem to be the result of things that happen to her rather than things she actually does; and whether the desires generated by one's interests turn out to be preposterous wishes or sensible wants would appear to be a matter of good or bad luck rather than good or bad reasoning.

However, this conclusion is unwarranted because it presupposes the false premise that if an event has not been directly willed it must be something that has simply happened to us. It is true that one cannot, for instance, just choose to believe such and such: belief cannot be the immediate object of any volition. But neither does it make sense to talk of a human being's beliefs as given facts about her, like morality, which she can do nothing about. Beliefs are the product of mental activities which are to a large extent within the control of the believer.[10] An individual can make a conscious effort to face disagreeable facts or engage in wish-fulfilling fantasies instead, and the course she takes will have a deep influence on what she ultimately comes to believe. We are all aware (or should be) of the extent to which our wishes about the world and ourselves can distort our beliefs, and the extent of this distortion is not an immutable fact of normal human nature. We can do something about it. Thus one might say, stretching language a bit, we choose our beliefs in part indirectly insofar as we choose to curb the natural tendency to fantasize. If that is so then an individual can exercise the same capacity for choice in the shaping of her interests (and hence in the shaping of the self) because interests entail beliefs of a certain sort. Admittedly, if I became convinced that I should repudiate as a temptation what I have hitherto held as an interest, some residual attraction towards its object inevitably will persist, but even that is something which the choices I make can normally arrest or sustain. I can passively indulge longings for what I have realized to be evil, unworthy, or futile, or else I can channel my energies and attention on other directions; and to the extent that a sense of personal fulfilment is thereby achieved, the pull of my previous interests will correspondingly diminish.

But this is perhaps too general to be revealing. It might help to sketch some of the broad considerations which can be brought to bear as one tries to create a meaningful life in a spirit of fidelity to the truth. For example, such a life requires the individual to maintain a certain level of concord among rival interests and in the relations they bear to other propensities. The importance of this need becomes obvious if we think of a life as analogous to a poem or story. A poem is not a random assemblage of individually significant words: its significance depends on a purpose (or purposes) which integrates the particular words into a coherent whole. Without this unity, a poem becomes pointless, despite the fact that it might contain arresting images or phrases. In a similar way, it would appear that a meaningful life must approximate a condition of internal concord for such a life is not a random sequence of independently valuable experiences and achievements. Rather, its meaning is located in certain continuities of direction, especially those afforded by our deeper and more enduring interests. To be sure, it is dangerous to press this point too hard. Significant poems, even great ones, may be pretty disorderly, and meaningful lives may be shaped by rather untidy motivational structures. But there is a point at which looseness of structure becomes no structure at all, and with this loss there is also a collapse of meaning.

Imagine someone who cannot or will not resolve a conflict between two radically opposing commitments. Her deep and abiding interest in things of the spirit (or what she convinces herself is such an interest) has led her to apply for membership in an especially ascetic order of nuns. Meanwhile, she is intensely absorbed in an adulterous relationship. The flagrant incoherence in this woman's life makes it seem reasonable to say that she does not know or has not decided who she is at all. And so long as her discrepant loyalties persist, her life, as a whole, is surely devoid of meaning. It might be possible to flesh out the details of this case so that the woman could be aptly seen as an essentially admirable person, who had become the victim of circumstances largely beyond her control. But another and more obvious way of elaborating this story would make her situation an object of justifiable contempt rather than compassion. For what frequently lies behind this kind of radical motivational conflict is a sort of culpable stupidity. By embellishing her case in this way, the woman becomes guilty of an abject failure to face the circumstances of her life in a spirit of truthfulness. Her plight is the stuff of comedy rather than tragedy. Her declarations of helplessness with respect to her dilemma would merely be rationalizations for her desire to have the best of both worlds without accepting the costs of either. In that event, the lack of any stable meaning in her life would be her own doing – she is responsible for her own predicament.

This kind of radical internal conflict is perhaps rather rare. Not many of us are so unfortunate or so culpably stupid as to suffer this particular fate. But friction between rival interests is an almost ubiquitous experience, its minimization an essential human task. My interests in philosophy and my family impose competing demands upon my time and energies. The result is that I am never quite the family man or the philosopher I would ideally like to be. A condition of perfect harmony between one's interests in doubtless almost impossible. Indeed, the illusion that it is possible may be quite disastrous. But it is feasible to reduce friction to a modest level, and calmly accept what remains irreducible. This achievement presupposes the possession of precisely the same spirit of truthfulness as the resolution of more fundamental conflicts. One has to anticipate, without gratifying illusions, how possible ways of balancing conflicting commitments may affect the self and others, discern one's own priorities clearly, and see how one may limit the damage that must be done.

Other considerations will weigh heavily with anyone who strives to shape her motivational structure in what I call a realistic manner. Facts about one's nature and situation – emotional idiosyncracies, strengths, and deficiencies of talent – as well as other features of one's temperament or abilities must be taken into account. In deciding to put this commitment at the centre of a motivational structure or that one at the periphery, in embracing this as an interest and shunning that as a mere source of temptation, we can respect or fail to respect the reality that circumscribes our choices. A child with no natural affinity for science may assiduously cultivate an "interest" in the subject. In a lucid moment she would have to admit that her studies afford nothing she could seriously endorse as intrinsically valuable. But she desperately avoids that realization because she wants to fulfil her parents' ambition that she become a scientist. Self-deception may work in the other direction as well. A child who can feel something of the wonder of scientific practice at the early stages of study may deny that sense of wonder because science is not approved by the right peer group.

If there is gross self-deception about what naturally attracts one, one's talents, and so forth, any happiness achieved will hardly be secure. But if happiness could be maintained in such a situation, a life of this kind would still be an appalling failure judged by any even faintly familiar conception of a life's meaning. Suppose someone devotes her life to writing bad novels which no one is foolish enough to publish. She is happy, however, because she has deceived herself into thinking that her novels are masterpieces which will be appreciated in a more artistically advanced age. In the last stage of a terminal illness her self-deception unravels, and she realizes that her novels were trash because her talents were so parlous. If we look at this life from the perspective of a sincere utilitarian, it was an impressive success. A period of prolonged happiness was offset by a bout of despair at the end of her life, but the brevity of the latter could not detract much from the overall extent of success in the form of happiness. Yet this is surely a very strange perspective – at least it is strange outside the esoteric context of moral theory. We expect this woman to feel that her entire life had been a terrible failure because it had been founded upon a lie. She had been living in a dream world, and the happiness her illusions gave her would seem quite worthless. Further, since self-deception voided her life of significance, she must bear some responsibility for its meaninglessness. If only she had resisted the pull of her own fantasies she might have lived a genuinely fulfilled life, anchored in the truth of her nature and circumstances.

At the beginning of this chapter I distinguished two closely connected aspects to the regulation of the will: the task of giving shape to one's motivational structure, and the control of occurrent desires generated by that structure as one makes particular choices. I have been talking about the first task. I now will briefly discuss the second.

It is well to remember that however faithfully one's motivational structure reflects the spirit of truthfulness, it will include constituents one disowns in one sense, but must acknowledge in another. That is to say, it will include proclivities – propensities one sees as persistent sources of temptation. So the problem of coping with the occurrent desires generated by these propensities remains with us, irrespective of how realistic we are in structuring our basic commitments.

In order to understand the application of realism to this problem it will help to make a further distinction between desires which become volitions and those which do not. If I experience temptation, I necessarily desire to do what temptation urges. The experience may be very like something that just happens to me because I surely cannot help feeling tempted from time to time to act contrary to what I know to be for the best. Yet when desire manifests itself in volition – when we will this rather than that – it is very implausible to think of the desires which motivate us as things that just happen to us. We might ask a frightened and inexperienced high-diver who is about to climb the divingboard if she wanted to avoid diving. She could sincerely deny this despite her intense inclination to beat a hasty retreat. This is a conceivable situation since it is possible that what she desires most deeply is to become an accomplished diver. And so diving is what she wills. Such desires – and they are the morally interesting ones since they are what normally motivate our actions – certainly are subject to rational control.

How is this possible? An illuminating way of describing the experience of succumbing to temptation is to say that we lost sight of what we truly valued. Naturally we think of this sort of lapse as something we can be held responsible for. One cannot help feeling attracted sometimes to what is evil or imprudent, say, but one can normally prevent the disregard of moral and prudential concerns to which these feelings often lead. Indeed, one can often remember a moment when one quite deliberately lost sight of such concerns, turning the mind away from them to contemplate the object of temptation without misgivings. In other words, one can allow a state of mind to come into being in which what one wills is what one feels tempted to do. The struggle of resisting temptation is simply the attempt to prevent this mental state from arising by focusing attention upon those interests to which it runs counter. It is easy to see how this might work in the case of the high-diver. One imagines her trying to anticipate the pride she will feel if the dive is successful, or rehearsing the sequence of actions she will go through as she dives and falls into the water without mishap. These thoughts nourish her will to dive. At the same time, she pushes from consciousness all thoughts that would nourish fear, and so long as she can push them away, temptation can be held in check. Although prayer may have certain metaphysical drawbacks, the value religious people attach to it reflects the important fact that it is only by a sort of mental discipline, an orientation of the mind towards the objects of our deeper aspirations which does not always come easily to us, that we can consistently live in a way that is true to the self.[11]

Strength of will presupposes the same spirit of truthfulness as the other aspects of realism I have discussed. I have to "see" my basic loyalties as such in situations where the pressure of temptation tends to blur the vision. Weakness of will, on the other hand, will commonly involve something at least closely akin to self-deception. The prospective high-diver who retreats to the lockerroom without getting wet may have succumbed to a fear she could not control. But then again she might not. The magnitude of her terror might have been something she herself precipitated by shifting attention away from what would have sustained the desire to dive and dwelling instead upon what would amplify her fears. She might have *indulged* in thoughts of broken limbs, wheel-chairs, and the like instead of being merely overwhelmed by them. That is to say, she chose to think and feel as if she were someone to whom safety meant everything and becoming an accomplished high-diver counted for nothing. If this sort of thing happened very often, one might doubt the authenticity of the interest which temptation apparently subverts. But it is hardly necessary to argue that we do sometimes elect to "forget" about genuine and deep interests under the pull of opposing inclinations. When we do, it is not just a kind of self-deception or something closely resembling it. The meaning of our lives is also marred because we have betrayed what gives them their significance.

It might be granted that the concept of realism I have outlined encapsulates an important ideal. But why should we see it as an aspect of self-rule? There certainly are lapses from the spirit of truthfulness in the way we regulate our wills which are very obviously analogous to losses of political autonomy. The individual who wallows in a radical conflict of professed loyalties, pretending to be powerless to resolve the matter, fails to exercise self-government when she clearly might. She could be compared to the state which allows anarchy to erupt by refusing to exercise authority. Where there is no fundamental incoherence in someone's motivational structure, but the individual shows a weakness of will, the situation parallels a different kind of failure to sustain political self-rule. In this instance, the individual's situation echoes that of the state which yields some of its authority to a rebel faction within its territory. But there are also failures in the cultivation of realism which might be aptly viewed as excessive self-rule. Consider once again both the child who makes desperate though abortive efforts to become interested in science but will not acknowledge her failure, and the one who denies her natural attraction to scientific study. Their error seems to be a refusal to *submit* to the relevance of facts that cannot be wished away rather than a reluctance to take command of their desires where they could and should do so. Instead of imputing a lack of autonomy, one might ascribe to them a loss of authenticity because clearly these children, in a certain sense, are not being faithful to who they really are.

The notion of authenticity may well be important to understand what it is to choose realistically, but I do not believe its importance obliges us to admit that the metaphor of self-rule is not felicitous in some important cases of realism. What is common to all the lapses from realism I have discussed is the indulgence in self-deception or something very close to it. Regulating the will in the spirit of truthfulness is simply the disciplined suppression of self-deception in the way one comes to make choices. Self-deception is just a way of losing control of one's life. It is a mistake to think of it as something one might selectively practise on the basis of rational expectations about its consequences in this or that set of circumstances. "I see that what I did was base, ignoble, and so forth, but I shall feel better if I convince myself otherwise. So that's just what I shall do." This would be an incoherent thing to say because in recognizing self-deception for what it is, one makes the *deception* impossible. The individual who deceives herself about her interests or her natural affinities, for example, is surrendering to a mental tendency which, by its very nature, is largely unavailable to conscious control, and the frequency with which one surrenders to it will weaken the capacity to resist in the future. This makes surrendering a very dangerous business, at least in conditions where others cannot be expected to intervene benevolently when things go wrong. Today it may just protect our peace of mind from the disruption of disagreeable facts; tomorrow it may insulate us from truths essential to the meaning of our lives. Self-deception is like falling asleep while driving. The dreams may be nice but the risks are hardly worth it.

There is one last point I would like to stress before moving ahead. I have been talking about the disciplined avoidance of self-deception. This is not the same as the strenuous pursuit of self-knowledge. Deception is only one impediment to the achievement of knowledge, and self-deception is only one obstacle to self-knowledge. Perhaps many people fit the description of Thomas Gray's "mute inglorious Milton." But if they knew nothing of their immense native talents, self-deception might not explain their self-ignorance. They could live in an abundant spirit of truthfulness, but none of their experiences would disclose the powers that lie within. Granted, elements of self-knowledge are important if autonomy is to really flourish in our lives, and the avoidance of self-deception might not be sufficient for acquiring these. For that reason, those who want autonomy will be somewhat inclined to seek self-knowledge above and beyond what naturally accrues through the avoidance of self-deception. I use the weak phrase "somewhat inclined" advisedly. I have tried to show that realism is deeply connected with our capacity to create meaningful lives, at least given any familiar conception of what such a life would be. If we were to stipulate that realism requires the strenuous pursuit of self-knowledge, it would be at the expense of that connection as the following example will illustrate.

Imagine someone who is an ardent pursuer of self-knowledge. It is not enough that she does not deceive herself. She also has to uncover all hidden talents and aptitudes, and with that end in view she devotes much time to pursuing novel activities of various kinds. To uncover the roots of her emotional responses she spends many hours in minute self-scrutiny. She persistently asks herself certain questions: "Why did I do this? Why did I feel that?" Since people intimate with her and whose candour can be relied upon will be important resources in her search for self-knowledge, she will be inclined to question them closely about what they think of her.

It is hardly controversial to say that this imaginary figure is not a prepossessing one. But we must be careful when we try to identify what it is that makes her unprepossessing. It is not that too much self-knowledge is a bad thing. On the contrary, I would want to say that insofar as this woman's efforts yield self-knowledge, her success is to be valued. The real trouble lies elsewhere. In pursuing self-knowledge the value of the achievement may be outweighed by the costs of the pursuit, and where the pursuit becomes central to someone's life, that possibility would seem to become a virtual certainty. Inasmuch as I devote my energies to the disclosure of all my latent talents and aptitudes, I shall have less to spare for endeavours I am already familiar with and interested in, and the meaning I bestow upon my life through participation in these activities is thereby diminished. And if my engagements with the world are constantly interrupted by spells of self-absorption, I can discover little of the value these engagements might offer. For one thing, the uninhibited give and take of friendship will not be possible if intimacy is viewed primarily as a thing to be used to enhance self-knowledge. It is true that I have examined an extreme case, but its extremity is vital to my point. Moderation in the pursuit of self-knowledge is crucial if we are to create meaningful lives. But, on the other hand, moderation is no virtue in the avoidance of self-deception.

One of the strongest and most pervasive of human concerns is that which we have in eliciting from others favourable attitudes and feelings and avoiding the unfavourable ones. The desire is especially urgent where the relevant others are the object of one's love, admiration, or other such sentiments, because it is only in relationships where these sentiments are reciprocated that the need for community and intimacy can be met. I shall call this concern the social desire, and the various feelings and attitudes which are its object, positive regard.

The concept of the social desire applies to a vast and heterogeneous range of human propensities. The various specific dispositions which fall within its scope are means by which the meaning of our own lives comes to be bound up with the lives of others. Yet these desires are also means by which others may come to govern our lives in oppressive ways. Autonomy, it would appear, implies that the social desire is controlled in ways which can be psychologically difficult. Perhaps the clearest examples of autonomous conduct are found among those capable of allegiance to certain deeply held interests despite public scorn and isolation. Partly for this reason, autonomy is sometimes associated with fortitude.[12] Swimming against the stream is neither a necessary nor a sufficient condition of autonomy; though it is natural to think of autonomy as requiring a mind that is not merely realistic, but also socially independent in a way that enables the individual to willingly incur the hostility of the world where necessary.

Independent-mindedness is evinced by individuals in whose lives the social desire is checked in certain ways by other propensities. The desire for positive regard does not inhibit them from cultivating competing inclinations openly and with alacrity, even if some frustration of the social desire ensues. The degree of frustration one can tolerate is a variable matter: independence of mind, like realism, is very much a matter of degree. Where the level of tolerance is extremely low, we may impute to the individual not merely a poor approximation to the ideal of realism, but also a failure to satisfy the minimal conditions of choice and responsibility. This imputation might be defensible, say, when explaining the behaviour of a deranged zealot who obsessively seeks the approval of a charismatic spiritual leader. Yet in other cases, which are not only conceivable but also familiar, an individual may show a degree of dependent-mindedness which indicates a serious deficiency in autonomy, even though no deficiency in realism can be clearly established. The following example will illustrate this point.

Suppose a young woman finds herself deeply attracted to a form of life outside the closed religious community in which she has been reared. Her parents would reject her completely if she left the community, and since she believes estrangement from them would be unbearable, she acquiesces to their demands. It is wrong to assume that her decision is an unrealistic one. It might not have involved self-deception or any other failure to take due cognizance of relevant facts. She could have very good reason to think that estrangement would be unbearable, however hard she tried to cope with it, and good reason to believe that a life within her community would be somewhat better than bearable. So we might agree that the decision was a highly realistic one. But it hardly follows that the decision was highly autonomous because her conduct reveals a kind or degree of dependence not consistent with being strongly autonomous. It is a platitude that autonomous persons have minds of their own. In the present case, the young woman does not really have a mind of her own, or enough of one, because her parents possess so much of it.

If we are to conceive of autonomy in the manner I have suggested, then what can be said about its value? That question has to be answered in a way that gives us persuasive grounds to want autonomy for ourselves and our children. Otherwise, autonomy (in my sense) could not provide any resolution to the difficulties surrounding the value of liberty noted at the end of the preceding chapter, and the educational recommendations, derived from the ideal of self-rule, which I shall make in succeeding chapters, would have no appeal.

If we try to justify autonomy instrumentally, we will encounter much the same difficulties which beset Mill's attempt to justify liberty as a means to happiness. The chief point is that although in certain conditions autonomy clearly does contribute to happiness, in very many it does not, and in still more its contribution is unclear. It might be conceded that where people are placed in circumstances where there is extensive freedom, and hence the opportunity (as well as the burden) of creating the meaning of their lives, their happiness is likely to be fragile at best if they have little realism or independence of mind. But this cannot justify autonomy because it can still be asked why these circumstances are desirable in the first place. No doubt tradition-directed cultures cannot be regained in full measure. Yet it can be argued that people would be more contented in communities where traditions left far less room for individual discretion than they now do, and the development of tradition-directed communities which fit that description does not appear to be an unfeasible aspiration.

J.P. White has tried to take a familiar way around the impasse created by a failure to justify autonomy in instrumental terms. He has argued that the desirability of autonomy can be established by virtue of the alleged absence of ethical experts to whose wisdom we should defer when our desires conflict or we encounter moral dilemmas. This move is familiar because philosophers have tried to justify a range of liberal policies and practices – freedom, tolerance, and democracy[13] – on the basis of the alleged unavailability of moral expertise. All these arguments are unsuccessful. I will grant that if there were no expertise in this area we would have to agree with White that "educators have no good reason to bring up their pupils believing that they should rely on authority when faced with conflicting desires." But our agreement would not commit us to his conclusion that "encouraging autonomous choice is not at all an arbitrary imposition on a pupil."[14] For if ethical expertise is just a Platonic figment, we have no reason to believe that pupils who have become highly autonomous will be better placed to make the right decision than those who unthinkingly follow orders. On the assumption that there is no ethical expertise, the encouragement of autonomy is just as arbitrary as the fostering of mindless obedience.

Let me elaborate this point. The concept of ethical expertise is valid if there is knowledge or other personal attributes not easily come by, either because their acquisition requires protracted and serious effort or special talents, and if their acquisition will put the individual in a better position to make the right decision than she would otherwise have been, at least with other things being equal. (Expertise in this area does not imply infallibility, nor does it require the elevation of anyone to elite political status, though the unfortunate association of ethical expertise with Plato's political theory has obscured these obvious facts.) White appears to reject ethical expertise because he believes that there are no people who possess the necessary knowledge or at least, if there were, we could not know who they were. Suppose he is right about this. Since *neither* autonomy nor mindless deference to authority could be shown to facilitate the right decision, whichever course we encouraged our children to take would be arbitrary, at least in the absence of any additional argument to show that one was preferable to the other. And the rejection of ethical expertise gives us no reason to favour freedom over constraint, tolerance over intolerance, or democracy over other types of government. These are moral preferences which have to be justified by moral reasons, and if we could not tell who was well situated to discern such reasons, that would not give us any reason for this preference as opposed to that one.

I want to maintain that autonomy is intrinsically valuable. Before presenting my case it is worth pointing out that arguments concerning intrinsic values are not decisive. When we try to establish instrumental or constitutive values, we focus upon certain empirical or conceptual relations; appeals to evaluative intuitions may be inconspicuous, though they will be there nonetheless. In discussion about intrinsic values, appeals to intuition are apt to loom large, but that does not mean we cannot argue our case. We can explore the implications of accepting or rejecting this or that judgment of intrinsic value, and, as the exploration unfolds, some will become increasingly appealing and others, starkly implausible. For instance, utilitarians who claim that only happiness (or preference satisfaction) is intrinsically valuable have tried to allay the doubts of others by showing that utilitarianism does not warrant ludicrous or repugnant policies, as their opponents argue, but rather makes better sense of our considered moral judgments than alternative conceptions.[15] Even if utilitarians were entirely successful in these efforts – and I do not think they are – their defence is not impregnable because it is conceivable, if not probable, that some reasonable persons would reject many of our considered moral judgments. But the utilitarian argument could, nonetheless, be *persuasive* for reasonable people in the world as we know it and that, as many philosophers since Aristotle have known, is usually the most we can expect of reasoning about such matters.

The interests of human beings frequently presuppose that things have intrinsic value other than states of mind. If a scientist said that physics mattered just for the agreeable experiences induced by its study and facilitated by its technological applications, she would strike me as someone with an oddly narrow view of the point of scientific study. But even if one agreed with her position, it would still have to be acknowledged that it does not represent any massive consensus about the value of physics. Significantly, it is uncontroversial to prize something just for its experiential payoff only in the relatively trivial context of the things we like as opposed to the things we are interested in. "Ice-cream is good just because of the pleasure it gives us" is something that virtually all ice-cream lovers can assent to without hesitation. Parallel claims about the value of philosophy or religion could hardly command the same degree of assent among their devotees.

I suggest that one major reason for recoiling from the prospect of evaluating everything in terms of experiential payoff is the fact that we are inclined to regard the exercise of autonomy as intrinsically valuable to a high degree. It is not hard to imagine a world in which all the experiences we treasure are achieved in full measure but where we are nonetheless deprived of control of our own lives. This possibility is vividly presented in a famous argument of Robert Nozick. He asks us to imagine that we all could plug into a machine that would stimulate in the brain whatever experiences we desire.[16] The point of the example is to bring into relief a widely held but often unnoticed intuition: there are intrinsically valuable things in our lives which are not experiences. If the joys of winning a game, making love, or making scientific discoveries could be mechanically produced, one could still regard these experiences as a poor substitute for the reality of victory, love-making, or scientific discovery, even if the joys were the same in either case. Many of us would be deeply averse to being plugged into the experience machine for any substantial portion of our lives, and that aversion only makes sense if we believe that not only experiences bear intrinsic value.

The intuition Nozick's example initially reveals is too general to support the thesis we are concerned with. Even if there are intrinsically valuable things other than experiences, it does not strictly follow that personal autonomy is one of them. But Nozick goes on to consider ways in which the machinery might be modified to assuage our intuitive aversion, and in so doing clarifies the basis of our aversion. Suppose we hesitate to use this machine just because we want to *be* certain kinds of people or produce certain effects in the world. Then our aversion to the machine should disappear if we also had access to a transformation machine, which could turn us into whatever kind of person we wished to become, and a results machine, which could change the world in any direction we pleased. A life devoted to exploiting these machines should impress us as a supremely desirable one. But it does not. Why? "What is most disturbing about (these machines) is their living our lives for us ... Perhaps what we desire is to live (an active verb) ourselves, in contact with reality. (And this, machines cannot do *for* us.)"[17]

We live our own lives to the extent that the experiences we have, the kind of persons we become, and the changes we make to the world flow from the exercise of personal autonomy. Nozick forces us to imagine a world in which the objects of our various desires have been severed from that source, and it turns out to be a world in which something we prize has been lost. To be sure, the transformation machine would enable one to become a highly autonomous person, while the others might be used to have only those experiences and produce just those results compatible with a highly autonomous character. But our lives could not involve the *exercise* of autonomy, except on those occasions when we unplugged ourselves, and for that reason they would not be lives in which the ideal of autonomy truly flourished.

Nozick's argument hinges upon an extravagant bit of science fiction. The fact that it does has provoked an obvious counterargument from Peter Singer, a prominent contemporary utilitarian. Singer points out that our intuitions about what should be done in odd circumstances are hardly a reliable indicator of what we value, upon reflection, in the lives we actually lead. If the orthodox utilitarian response to the experience machine (Let's plug in!) and favourable responses to the other machines seem foreign to us, this is not necessarily because they run counter to deeply entrenched intuitions of intrinsic value. The right response to a bizarre situation may be a bizarre one, according to Singer, and our unease at the thought of plugging in may simply stem from the recognition that it would be bizarre to do so.[18] But there is a vital difference between the intuition that it would be wrong or bad to plug in and the feeling that it would be *merely* strange. The counterargument will not hold if we are confident that we have the former rather than the latter intuition. I for one find nothing especially strange about the prospect of plugging in. The charms of this kind of machinery should not be altogether foreign to a culture which thrives, after a fashion, on the highly passive pleasures of television viewing. Further, the examples are bizarre only because they separate things which are deeply entangled in the ordinary course of our lives – the experiences we have, the kind of people we become, the changes we make to the world, and the exercise of autonomy. It is precisely because these things are ordinarily entangled that our judgments about their value are liable to become blurred. Even if the attempt to clarify and refine our ultimate evaluations leads us to engage in outlandish thought experiments, the self-knowledge we gain therein may have important applications to our lives as they are presently constituted. A world in which Nozick's science-fiction machinery is available, *without* costs which even a utilitarian would balk at, is not just around the corner; but we nonetheless do inhabit a world where the values he forces us to discriminate, though hard to disentangle, are not so harmoniously combined that sacrifices in one area will not often be the price of gains in another.

Further considerations can be adduced in defence of autonomy as a personal ideal. Autonomy is essential to the exercise of moral virtue and the achievement of justifiable self-respect; and because these things are plausibly regarded as very weighty intrinsic values, autonomy can be seen, with equal plausibility, as a very weighty constitutive good. (It would be possible to conduct thought experiments to support these judgments of intrinsic value, but since I think their appeal is fairly obvious, I shall not press the matter.) The conceptual connections which make autonomy a constitutive good yield an especially strong justification because it is not the case that only minimal autonomy is necessary to evince moral excellence or achieve a robust and well-grounded sense of self-respect; it is rather the case that the degree to which these intrinsic values are realized necessarily depends on the degree autonomy is realized.

Whatever conception of the virtuous character one espouses – and I do not assume that only one reasonable conception is available – there is good reason to believe that it is connected with the notion of autonomy in the manner I have suggested. In the first place, the extent to which we are realistic necessarily has a bearing on the extent to which we live virtuously. A virtuous person aspires to live a morally excellent life, but because she has propensities which are apt to conflict with that aspiration, she will be tempted to act upon them when conflict arises and pretend that she has done nothing wrong. Injustice to a stranger might be passed off as a matter of permissible partiality for a friend, cruelty can be viewed as giving others their just deserts, and so on. These rationalizations are not necessarily just retrospective wish-fulfilment: they also enable us to conceive our options *prior* to action in such a way that their true significance is obscured and the pull of the moral interest is obviated. One exercises virtue to the degree that one can resist temptation, and one can do that only to the extent that the will is regulated in a realistic fashion.

In many cases, there are also compelling grounds to believe a large measure of independence of mind is needed if virtue is to prevail. The demands of morality and our desires for the positive regard of others may coincide in the ordinary course of events, but things do not always work out so happily. If I am driven by a desire to be loved and admired by my child at all costs, I shall not be a morally successful parent. Similar problems arise in the realm of public morality where acting justly, for instance, might sometimes alienate one from those whose love or respect one cherishes. To be sure, people who are compassionate, just, and the like, may be deeply absorbed in the satisfactions of intimacy and community; but their absorption has to be qualified and sometimes countered by the moral interest. There should be nothing surprising about this. Parents who selflessly encourage their daughter to pursue a career far from her home because it is to her advantage do not necessarily desire close contact with their child any less than other parents. And those who have heroically opposed unjust wars conducted by their own countries have often been ardently patriotic. In circumstances of this kind, virtue would be impossible in the absence of a high degree of independence of mind.

In order to grasp the connection between autonomy and self-respect it is necessary to distinguish the latter from the wider concept of self-esteem. Although the distinction I shall draw is at best faintly evident in everyday usage and is ignored in the most influential philosophical analysis of self-respect,[19] it enables us to sort out two importantly different concepts.

If someone had devoted her life to perpetrating the most terrible crimes, we would certainly want her to recognize the evil of her deeds and character. However, it does not follow that we would regard her (or would want her to regard herself) as worthless. Like parental love, our moral attitude towards other persons has a certain constancy in the face of fluctuations in the value of their actions and character, and that constancy only makes sense if we assume that other persons have a value apart from these things. It would be wrong to torture the most evil person who has ever lived, but the idea that one could do wrong to something entirely worthless is unintelligible. All persons have a justifiable sense of self-esteem, at least to the extent that they recognize their worth as persons.

Yet being a person is not something one can take credit for outside of science-fiction cases. What justifiably contributes to self-esteem does not necessarily make a fitting contribution to self-respect. My self-esteem is determined by the value I attach to what I am and have done; my self-respect is determined by the extent to which I believe I can take credit for the value of what I am and have done. Although the perpetrator of terrible crimes can appropriately prize her own personhood and to that degree have self-esteem, she could have no justifiable self-respect because what she has made of her life is thoroughly evil.

The next move is obvious. We can take credit for what is valuable in our lives, and thereby enhance the degree to which we have justifiable self-respect, only to the extent that we create this value through the exercise of personal autonomy. Someone who had lost the ability to walk and then recovered it through heroic exertions has grounds for self-respect because her achievement depends upon aspects of self-rule such as resoluteness of purpose in the face of temptation. On the other hand, the ability to walk is typically something that cannot legitimately bolster one's self-respect because its achievement typically has nothing to do with self-rule. Our preoccupation with self-respect stems from the fact that we not only want to be the bearers of valuable attributes but also want to have a substantial and creative role in the development and expression of those attributes. Undoubtedly, certain people do not have that desire. But their existence gives those who have it no reason to suppress the desire and no reason to refrain from encouraging it in the education of our children.

The argument for autonomy via moral virtue and self-respect reinforces the conclusion of Nozick's thought experiment. Further, it clarifies the basis of our antipathy to the machines he asks us to imagine. It is not the case, after all, that we could repudiate autonomy and have everything else we desire because autonomy is partly constitutive of moral virtue and self-respect – at least two other things we value deeply.

So far in this chapter I have been talking about autonomy rather than freedom. But at the end of chapter one I claimed that freedom was partly constitutive of a life in which the ideal of autonomy is instantiated. I now wish to explain and defend that claim.

I might enjoy all the liberty anyone could reasonably want, but I may only evince the modicum of realism and independence of mind required by the capacity for choice. Yet my freedom is surely one of the necessities of a life in which autonomy can genuinely thrive. In order to see this, one might consider the predicament of individuals whose options are severely circumscribed by the familiar techniques of totalitarian government. The shadowy presence of the secret police, the use of informants, systematic deception through the mass media, and the like, are all ways of preventing citizens from acting or even thinking in ways unacceptable to the authorities. Within the realm of conduct which has any political significance – and of course that covers just about everything – the paucity of open options means that individuals have the power to decide what to do only on relatively unimportant matters. That is to say, there is negligible room to exercise autonomy. It is possible even in these dire straits for an individual to show remarkable autonomy as, for example, in the conduct of political dissidents. However, cases of that kind presuppose the state's failure to destroy political freedom altogether. At any rate, lives in which autonomy (as an ideal) can scarcely be expressed except in isolated acts of heroism are not the same as those in which it can prosper within a manifold range of open options.

It may be granted that in some areas, such as political activity, the tight connection between liberty and autonomy I have been stressing does hold, and hence, that freedom does bear constitutive value within these specific areas. But to claim that all liberties have constitutive value through their link to autonomy might strike one as grossly pretentious in light of the paltry choices which are ubiquitous in the doings and omissions of our daily lives. When I choose this product rather than that one from the shelves of the supermarket, it is not with a vivid sense that I am expressing myself as a realistic and independent-minded agent. If I did my shopping on a day when stocks were somewhat depleted so that my possibilities of choice were unexpectedly narrow, I would not feel that my dignity qua a self-determining agent had been compromised. This suggests that our autonomy is much more urgently at stake in some liberties than in others, and that is a vitally important point to which I shall return shortly. What I want to consider now is whether or not admittedly trivial freedoms have some constitutive value in relation to autonomy, and the fact that they do is of some consequence.

If laws were introduced depriving us of a range of open options which, taken individually, we would regard as trivial – options pertaining to the wearing of certain clothes or the eating of certain foods, say – we could have reason to oppose them as a significant encroachment upon our autonomy. The totalitarian society depicted in Orwell's *1984* is degrading not just because it is a place in which individuals no longer make any "big decisions" concerning political or religious affiliation, the selection of a spouse or a career, and the like. Its oppressive character is also evident in the way the minute detail of citizens' lives is taken out of their hands. If one focused upon a tiny patch of colour in a great painting it would be odd to say that it expressed the artist's creativity. Nevertheless, it is the details of execution as well as larger matters concerning the style, content or scale of the work which attest to the artist's creative powers. Likewise, my most trivial actions and omissions enter into the fabric of a life which, taken in its entirety, reveals whatever success I have in meeting the demands of autonomy; and if I look at my life in that way, it is clear that the mundane as well as the momentous possibilities of choice contribute to my achievement.

A further objection may be raised here: because constraints which limit freedom are often necessary to protect or enhance autonomy, freedom and autonomy must be fundamentally distinct values. Rousseau's choice between residing in Paris or Geneva is a case in point. Paris offered more freedom but also temptations which threatened to undermine the autonomous character; in Geneva there was less freedom but also a more protected environment.[20] This does not mean that there is a radical cleavage between freedom and autonomy as values, a cleavage which would oblige us to deny that any liberty has constitutive value in relation to self-rule. For a life in which the ideal of autonomy is substantially realized requires that realism and independence of mind be exercised and not merely possessed, even though opportunities to exercise them will often endanger their continued possession. There should be nothing surprising about this since precisely the same point can be made about other personal ideals. Courageous actions may redound to the agent's disadvantage so severely that she loses her nerve entirely and becomes incapable of courage in the future. The environment which provides the best protection against risks of that kind will not be the best choice if we want courage to prosper because maximum protection would severely inhibit courageous actions. For parallel reasons, maximum protection against choices which diminish our autonomy will not be compatible with having adequate scope for its expression. By prizing autonomy, one will sometimes be led to favour protective measures, all things considered; but that is entirely consistent with our always having *a* reason to favour liberty, though not always a decisive reason, by virtue of its connection to self-rule.

If all open options give some scope for the exercise of autonomy, and if autonomy has the value I have assigned to it, then there is a case for a strong presumptive principle of liberty. That is to say, we should strive to maximize freedom and only settle for less than we might have where a reason of sufficient weight defeats the presumption in favour of maximizing freedom. I discussed the presumptive principle at the end of the previous chapter, interpreting it as an affirmation of the intrinsic value of freedom and showed that under that interpretation, it could not resolve the difficulties of a purely instrumental theory of the value of liberty. But we can also construe the principle as an acknowledgment of the constitutive value of freedom, and, understood along those lines, escape the difficulties of the instrumental theory. In order to establish that conclusion, however, we need to examine just what it means to "maximize" freedom.

Consider the following argument Charles Taylor presents in a highly incisive essay. (I should hasten to add that Taylor does not want us to accept the argument. He merely uses it for purposes of illustration, though the point he wishes to illustrate is somewhat different than the one I intend to make.[21]) Albania is a free country. Indeed, it is more free than Britain. Religious practices are all prohibited in Albania, but there are far fewer traffic lights in the streets of Tirana than in London. The loss of freedom in the religious realm is outweighed by the greater liberty Albanians enjoy in their activities as pedestrians and motorists.

If anyone were insane enough actually to endorse this argument, the obvious response would be to say that because religious liberty is infinitely more important than fewer constraints upon driving and walking, Albania cannot be freer than Britain, at least if that is the best that can be said about the liberty Albanians enjoy. Yet a literal reading of the argument would suggest that the obvious response contains a fallacy. The argument is supposed to establish that there is *more* freedom in Albania than in Britain. Isn't this different from attempting to show that it contains more *important* freedoms? The art gallery which contains the best paintings is not necessarily the one that has the most paintings; and similarly, the most free nation may not be the one which protects the most important liberties. But qualitative and quantitative judgments about freedom cannot be prized apart as tidily as this. It is precisely the interdependence of such judgments which makes the obvious rejoinder a telling one.

The things we are free to do are options we are free to take or forego. As Isaiah Berlin has said, these are not discrete entities like apples (or paintings for that matter) which are readily discriminated and enumerated in the same way by anyone who possesses the relevant concepts.[22] What we count as a distinct option is contingent upon what we regard as an actual or possible desire worth distinguishing from others in the context we are considering, and in making these discriminations we are inevitably guided by some standard of value other than the bare notion of freedom. It is the relevance of such a standard of value which makes the defence of Albania as a freer country than Britain so patently absurd. To take the position that the loss of religious freedom could be outweighed by less constrained driving conditions presupposes a grotesquely eccentric view of what matters in our lives. In order to justify the position, one would have to argue, for instance, that being at liberty to drive without the interruption of many traffic lights gives one room to express more of those desires that are important in human life than being free to engage in public worship. Now if we shatter the defence of Albania as a freer country than Britain by exposing its ludicrous assumptions about what matters in human lives, then we have refuted what is *ostensibly* a purely quantitative judgment about freedom (Albania is more free than Britain) on the basis of a judgment about the value of different liberties (religious freedom is more important than unconstrained driving conditions).

Taylor's facetious argument shows that the choices we make in order to maximize freedom will be guided by some extrinsic standard of value. If the presumptive principle is construed as an affirmation of the constitutive value of freedom in relation to autonomy, then to maximize freedom is to enlarge the scope one has to exercise autonomy. In other words, the ideal of autonomy provides the relevant standard of value. To be sure, the ideal entails that all liberties possess *some* constitutive value, but it also provides a basis for those judgments about the comparative value of different possible liberties which the presumptive principle obliges us to make.

By prizing autonomy for ourselves and others, we will take some actual and possible desires to be especially important, and naturally regard open options corresponding to these as adding more to our freedom than other possible liberties. I have argued that autonomy consists in the regulation of the will, and that this control is rooted in our motivational structures, at the heart of which lie our personal interests. The interests we choose to cultivate are the foundation of individual self-rule in much the same way that the constitution and the most cherished policies of an independent state are fundamental to its sovereignty. A state forced to revise its constitution at the behest of a powerful neighbour would suffer a far greater blow to its independence than one which merely had to give way on some minor point in its trading policies. Similarly, if I were a strongly autonomous agent and subject to constraints which utterly thwarted me in the expression of my deepest interests, I would suffer a greater violation of autonomy than if I were constrained in acting upon some mild and fleeting predilection.

But just because someone is deprived of the freedom to express even a consuming personal interest, it does not strictly follow that her range of open options has significantly been diminished. A heroin addict's only interest is in getting high, though if we prevented her from doing so it could not, in the ordinary course of events, be claimed that our actions were a serious violation of her freedom. One can cogently argue on the basis of widely known facts about heroin addiction that an individual will not indulge in it unless she has lapsed grievously from the ideal of autonomy. By stopping her from using heroin, we do not prevent her from exercising autonomy to any significant extent; and, given that autonomy provides the relevant standard of value, we do not diminish her liberty to such an extent. In estimating the contribution to someone's overall freedom of this or that possibility of choice, one has to bear in mind not only its relation to the agent's current interests, but also the degree to which actually taking the option would instantiate autonomy. Many other cases could illustrate the relevance of this consideration, such as the laws against selling oneself into slavery which Mill was anxious to justify. But I trust that it is unnecessary to belabour the point.

Another relevant factor comes into focus if we consider again the problem of religious liberty in contemporary Albania. It is reasonable to assume that after decades of living without religious freedom, and with relentless propaganda convincing individuals that they are better off without it, many Albanians would be untroubled by their deprivation. Indeed, they could find constraints upon religious practice a lot less bothersome than we find restrictions upon driving and walking in crowded western cities. Intuitively, however, it would appear that the loss of religious freedom still seriously detracts from their overall freedom, although the argument we have traced does not adequately support that intuition. Antireligious laws do not inhibit religiously apathetic Albanians from freely expressing any central constituent of their motivational structures. Furthermore, so long as they remain genuinely apathetic, the option of religious practice is not one that could exemplify a high degree of autonomy in their case. In other words, neither of the considerations I have adduced so far in explaining my interpretation of the presumptive principle of liberty can show why there is a substantial loss of freedom in this case.

The way around this impasse is not especially hard to find. Autonomy is an ideal which an individual can express by transforming an existing motivational system, in light of novel experiences and insights. A life in which autonomy flourishes does not merely permit self-rule according to an established scheme of values; it also affords the possibility of radical revisions to that scheme of values. Just as the sovereign state can rewrite its own constitution, abandon old ideals and policies, and embrace new ones, the autonomous agent can also recreate her motivational structure. If I am indifferent to religion and deprived of religious freedom, I am denied the possibility of self-transformation in one very central area of human activity, *even* if it is a possibility which I would never choose to exploit. For that reason, my deprivation seriously restricts the scope I have to exercise autonomy, and thereby seriously diminishes my freedom.

I would suggest that being denied some possibility of self-transformation limits the agent's freedom to the extent that: (i) the possibility of self-transformation could not be realized without restricting the individual's set of currently and autonomously valued open options and; (ii) the particular option is likely to be autonomously selected at some time in the future, or at least valued as a serious possibility of self-transformation, if the appropriate liberties were made available. This position can explain why a loss of religious liberty substantially diminishes freedom even where religious apathy prevails, without committing its adherents to supporting silly views about the significance of relevant constraints upon *any* conceivable self-transformation. First, the provision of religious freedom would not likely affect adversely one's existing set of autonomously valued liberties, at least outside of pretty outlandish imaginary situations. In the case of the Albanians, religious freedom could well cause discontent and anxiety in many quarters, but I am at a loss to see how it could significantly diminish the range of liberties which most Albanians currently and autonomously value. Second, obvious and indubitable facts about human beings indicate that religious liberty is something valuable from the viewpoint of autonomy, even where exclusively secular values obtain. We know that religious commitment is a highly pervasive phenomenon which may be absent at one point in an individual's life only to emerge vigorously later on, and when genuine faith does arise it transforms one's conception of life's meaning – service to God is not just one interest among others for those who truly believe. Even if one is a hard-nosed atheist, there is some reason to prize the liberty to practise religion as an insurance policy against the possibility of future conversion.

I have tried to show that by interpreting the presumptive principle of freedom as grounded in the value of autonomy, a justification can be given for why we cherish religious liberty and why it counts for so much in quantitative judgments about freedom. I suggest that if we pressed the matter further, the same interpretation of the presumptive principle could underwrite the special moral status of other deeply valued liberties such as freedom of speech and assembly, and the freedom to carve one's own, perhaps idiosyncratic, form of life within limits set by the legitimate interests of others. It would be a very lengthy task to work this suggestion out in detail, but the outlines of the argument are easily discerned. So long as autonomous people have interests, or are apt to acquire interests, which generate desires to persuade others of their views, to refine their thinking through dialogue, or to organize with like-minded persons in championing some common cause, then freedom of speech and assembly will be essential to their self-rule. There is also a large and varied range of forms of life which are ordinarily compatible with the demands of self-rule and due consideration of others' interests.Within that area, the varying natural predilections and talents of different persons will give rise to diverse and sometimes eccentric loyalties and aspirations; and if the autonomy of the individual is to be protected, freedom has to be safeguarded here as far as possible. It is for this reason that social diversity and individuality are so closely associated with freedom and autonomy in liberal political thought.

If we apply the presumptive principle according to what maximizes the scope for the exercise of autonomy, we can see why there should be substantial constancy in which liberties are morally privileged, given general facts about what is apt to interest autonomous agents in any tolerably familiar human community. Moreover, we can also be sensitive to intuitively important variations in what liberties are morally significant because there is notable variation in different lives in what matters to autonomous agents. A brief example may be helpful here. The freedom to hunt and trap does not count for much when we try to estimate the range of liberties which residents of New York city currently lack. It would count for a great deal, however, if we were considering the constraining effects of oil drilling upon the freedom of the Inuit in northern Canada. This argument has the advantage of being able to justify distinctions of this kind while at the same time supporting the virtually universal moral importance of some liberties. And given that autonomy has the value I have assigned to it, its connection with the presumptive principle provides a more appealing defence of freedom, and especially those liberties which seem to have a special moral status, than instrumental considerations alone can provide.

This chapter has traversed extensive philosophical territory at a brisk if not reckless pace. I have tried to clarify and justify an ideal of personal autonomy, and have presented this ideal as the linch-pin of a certain view about the value of freedom. I have also indicated how the notion of maximizing liberty should be interpreted according to that view of the value of freedom. All this is fundamental to the remaining chapters. If autonomy is an essential feature of the good life, then problems within educational policy have to be understood, at least in part, as questions about what would help or hinder students in learning to live autonomous lives. The arguments of the present chapter would lead one to expect that the maximization of freedom would be a cardinal consideration in answering these questions, and the arguments which follow will confirm that expectation.

CHAPTER THREE

Interests and Schooling

I hope to show that the school can make a vital contribution to an education for autonomy by providing a curriculum which develops students' interests. The chief advantage of such a curriculum is its power to enlarge the freedom of those subject to it. This rather controversial conclusion has to be defended against a number of counterarguments, which will occupy much of this chapter.

First, it is necessary to look at the grounds which philosophers of education have used to argue that children's interests are virtually irrelevant to the selection of curricular aims and content. I also have to contend with J.P. White's well-known position that a curriculum which gives overriding priority to breadth of understanding is necessary if autonomy is our goal. Finally, there is the objection that an interest-based curriculum of the sort I recommend, even if it serves the end of autonomy very well, does not contribute enough to the moral education of the child. In each case, I shall demonstrate that the counterargument has little or no force.

It is not hard to envisage a society that does not need schools. If the various outcomes of learning the young have to attain could all transpire through participation in the everyday life of the community, with perhaps a bit of direction from any adult who happens to be close at hand, then there would be no reason to institute the specific roles of teacher and student; and certainly there would be no need to formalize the endeavours of those who teach and those who learn in such a way that schools come into being. The concepts of teaching and schooling will be dealt with more fully in the following chapter. For now I want to stress the simple fact that schools are only necessary if there are important outcomes of learning that cannot be efficiently pursued without them. It would appear that these will be outcomes which are at least rather difficult to achieve without sustained and focused effort in specific learning activities, as well as persistent direction from someone who has the knowledge to set appropriate tasks and assess the merits of the learner's performance.

Obviously, there are important and even complex outcomes of learning in any society for which the school is not specifically suited. Oral mastery of a first language is the most obvious member of this category. Another plausible candidate is the acquisition of character traits. There is something intuitively ludicrous in the suggestion that we could become honest or courageous by attending lectures and lessons on the virtues, doing homework about them, and so on. The suggestion becomes no more palatable where autonomy rather than honesty or courage is to be the object of such efforts. It is true that the school's mission has often been to inculcate certain prized character traits, but that mission could only be embraced with any show of reason so long as the relevant traits were seen largely as the by-product of participation in the everyday life of the school. The master's directions were to be followed minutely, promptly, and without question, so the child would pick up a docile disposition while learning whatever was being explicitly taught. This "collateral learning," as Dewey called it[1] – contemporary writers prefer to talk about the hidden curriculum – has nothing uniquely to do with schooling. Character traits and the like may be powerfully encouraged by participation in other institutional settings as well. Indeed, given the often overwhelming influence of filial identification on the development of character, we have reason to be wary of ambitious claims about the efficiency of schooling in that context. For instance, if developing virtue is the central aim of moral education, then policies designed to change relationships between parents and children in certain ways – by reducing family violence, for example – are likely to be more important than whatever might happen in the classroom. Moreover, preoccupation with the latter may deflect attention from measures urgently required outside the school.

Nevertheless, the school has a distinctive and substantial role to play in the realization of autonomy. Undoubtedly, little or nothing is to be gained by making autonomy into an object of study, and it may well be true that schools cannot fulfill their role here unless conditions in other institutions, especially the family, are fairly propitious. But none of this undermines my case, which hinges on conceptual connections between the kind of learning the school is specifically equipped to provide and the flourishing of autonomy.

There is nothing unintelligible or even odd in the situation of someone who chooses or is able to choose in a highly autonomous fashion but has achieved little of the kind of learning for which schools are specifically suited. Imagine someone pursuing an austere rustic existence, not out of mindless fidelity to the traditions of her community, but because she has made a strongly autonomous choice to live that way. In imagining the ingredients of that choice, erudition or technical know-how are noticeably absent. If we imagine two agents opting for the same simple life – one an unschooled rustic, the other a polymath grown weary of academe, the scholarship of the polymath would hardly entail that her choice was more autonomous than the rustic's. Admittedly, if we conceived autonomy as exclusively manifest in highly examined lives, this conclusion would not hold. It could be argued that the unschooled rustic would not have the cognitive wherewithal to do enough or the right kind of examination. But I have already indicated why the notion of autonomy should not be restricted in this way.

It might still be true that the knowledge of the polymath will make her situation preferable, given the ideal of autonomy I have endorsed. Suppose we imagine the unschooled rustic as someone who endures rural simplicity only because she is tragically ignorant of her immense artistic abilities. We might agree that even a paragon of autonomy choosing under these cognitive constraints would not have chosen differently than the unschooled rustic. The trouble is that her ignorance reduces the eligibility of other options almost to a vanishing point, and among the precluded options is a form of life she would undertake eagerly if only she had a bit more self-knowledge. The knowledge of the polymath, on the other hand, yields an array of options unavailable to the unschooled rustic. She is able and free to do a host of things because of her academic accomplishments – read Dante, do complicated crossword puzzles, and so on – and these remain available for choice even if she foregoes them. Moreover, in pursuing knowledge in breadth and depth, she will have been able to explore her native inclinations and aptitudes quite thoroughly. She will also know much about the range of lives currently feasible in her society; and if she has kept self-deception in check, she will have a good inkling of what life best suits her nature. Even if the unschooled rustic and the polymath have been equally successful in avoiding self-deception, the latter will, under these circumstances, be less vulnerable to constraints upon choice caused by a lack of self-knowledge.

This example suggests some general observations about the relation between the kind of learning for which schools are especially suited and the cultivation of autonomy. First, though it is not logically inevitable that new academic achievements will increase our options, where there is an accession of ability in what we learn – and that is almost invariably true even where learning is abstruse and theoretical – then we are necessarily able to do what we could not do before; and in the absence of other constraints upon these options, we become free where we were previously unfree. Second, discovering some hidden ability in oneself, such as the native talents of a great artist, opens up options which a lack of self-knowledge had previously closed. In these ways, the acquisition of knowledge and skills can contribute to self-rule by increasing our freedom. Learning which has that consequence undoubtedly can take place without schooling, but it is hardly necessary to argue that the school might greatly facilitate its occurrence.

However, the truth here is a bit more complicated than these general remarks would indicate. Chapter two presented arguments linking the individual's interests, autonomy, and the extent of freedom. I maintained that if our concern for freedom is rooted in the ideal of autonomy, then the manner in which we estimate overall losses or gains in freedom will be determined by the extent to which different circumstances enhance or impede the exercise of autonomy. I also argued that as an individual's interests are the very foundation of her self-rule, constraints upon freedom will vary in severity according to how seriously they encroach upon the interests she has or could well come to have under certain conditions. Now I have just shown that the knowledge and skills schools provide can contribute to an education for autonomy by making us free to choose what we otherwise could not. But in light of the argument of chapter two, we should expect that the extent of the contribution to autonomy will only be substantial if what is learnt is closely connected with the learner's existing interests (if these are not in conflict with the claims of realism and independence of mind), or what could plausibly be regarded as possible future interests. Further reflection bears out this expectation.

The main reason for regarding the artistically talented rustic as less well situated to exercise autonomy than the polymath concerns the possible impact of ignorance on the emergence of new interests. We envisage the rustic as someone whose motivational structure would have been entirely different if only she had obtained a bit more knowledge about her own abilities and the personal fulfilment their development would have given her. There is an analogy here, with respect to the abridgement of autonomy, to the predicament of individuals who might well have developed profound religious or political commitments if they had not grown up in a society where all religious practices and political associations were suppressed. After all, if I suddenly discovered a new talent of no current interest to me and which could not reasonably be seen as the germ of some possible future interest – a talent for ear-wiggling, perhaps – its discovery would not constitute a momentous personal liberation. If we then imagine the unschooled rustic as someone deeply engaged in her simple existence, and who would opt for the same life even if she had all the educational advantages of the polymath, then her lack of those advantages does not carry as much weight when we appraise her situation by the standard of autonomy. It would remain true that the polymath is free to do things which are not options for the unschooled rustic because of her academic achievements. However, these options would not count for much for just the same reason that the liberties which Albanians enjoy, qua pedestrians and drivers, carry little weight when appraising their situation in terms of autonomy.

The educational significance of these remarks become clear if we consider the following case. Sharon graduates from secondary school having obtained a signally good education by conventional standards. She has as sound an understanding of the major academic disciplines as one could reasonably expect of a bright and industrious adolescent. But Sharon has virtually no interest in what she has been taught. Her success was motivated by a desire to excel in competition and win the approval of parents and other authority figures. What really matters to Sharon are things which her schooling has not touched at all: the emotional fulfilment of family life, the predictable pleasures of television drama, the esteem of those who wield authority over her, and so on. Some of what she has learnt at school relates to her interests, but only in a purely instrumental way: her academic qualifications help her to get a job, which in turn gives her the money to do some of the things she is interested in doing. A narrow vocational training or the right lottery ticket would have served the same end rather better. It is true that Sharon's schooling could have some intrinsic connection with interests she will come to acquire at a later date. Remembering a passage from *Hamlet* one had been obliged to learn by heart might inspire an interest in Shakespeare long after one has left the classroom, but empirical researchers are not needed to tell us that such things are most unlikely to occur to students who leave school without a spark of interest in Shakespeare.

Sharon's schooling could not have made much positive difference to her freedom to exercise autonomy. To be sure, her considerable academic knowledge enables her to do certain things, but because she is not interested in the options created by her schooling, and is likely to remain so, they do not significantly increase her freedom. Furthermore, what Sharon has been taught could not have helped to make her a more autonomous person. Realism is essentially a matter of striving to shape the will in light of the truth about one's nature and circumstances. If what Sharon is taught is without interest, then whatever truth it contains is without interest as well, and cannot even conceivably enrich that intense spirit of truthfulness, the essence of realism. For much the same reason, Sharon's schooling could not have helped to make her more independent-minded. Becoming independent-minded is necessarily a process of finding intrinsic value in one's world beyond the satisfaction of the social desire because only through interests which countervail its pull does independence of mind become possible. If nothing Sharon was taught at school interested her, then her schooling could not have helped to make her more independent-minded.

How is the fate of Sharon to be avoided in the kind of schoolin. we create for our children? The answer which may first spring to mind is that the school should be a place where children pursue their interests with the help of sympathetic and knowledgeable adults. But not only do we have no reason to suppose that pursuing one's interests, whatever they may be, will conduce to being a more autonomous person, their pursuit does not even necessarily produce anything of consequence in the way of greater knowledge and ability. Charles Clark and P.S. Wilson dispute the latter claim in their article,"On Children's Interests."[2] They maintain that interest in an object consists of wanting to learn more about it and the activity which expresses that desire is investigation. But obvious counter-examples can be brought to bear against this view. Children who are interested in cartoons will be absorbed in watching television from time to time, but they are hardly investigating as they gaze vacantly at the television screen, and it is unlikely that their absorption reflects a desire to *learn* about anything whatever.

If we focus upon cases of this kind, it becomes tempting to infer that the interests of children properly have nothing to do with an education for autonomy. That inference is a very dangerous mistake. This becomes clear once we appreciate the distinction between pursuing and developing an interest. In *pursuing* an interest, I engage in activities which, I believe, enrich the meaning of my life. The engagement might be devoid of any desire to understand my world more deeply, but that could not be true of situations

in which I was genuinely *developing* an interest. Professional philosophers of the mentally moribund variety might be pursuing an
interest in philosophy when they rehash old arguments or reiterate
hackneyed criticisms of academic adversaries. Yet the highly
circumscribed and repetitive nature of their efforts, and the intellectual torpor it reveals, makes it plain that they are no longer
significantly developing an interest in philosophy.

The development of an interest implies a deepening understanding of its object, as well as a desire for such understanding, and the
extent of the development is partly contingent on the depth of understanding one attains. It is only partly contingent because, as I
come to understand more about philosophy, I might realize that it
is really not the sort of thing sensible people should bother with at
all, and, as a result, my interest will naturally disappear rather
than develop. If development is to occur, my deepening understanding must lead me to discover more in the way of intrinsically
valued experience and achievement in philosophical activity. This
is certainly a slow and gradual process as a rule, but its character
is most clearly seen on occasions when it is achieved through a sort
of quantum leap. Suppose I had been contemptuous of all philosophy outside the Anglo-American tradition until a friend persuaded
me to attend a seminar on the work of some continental philosopher. I come away not only understanding more about philosophy,
but also (and as a result of my new understanding) with the conviction that there are fascinating philosophical problems of which I
had previously been unaware and unfamiliar and valuable approaches to the entire subject.

The development of my interest implies a context where the
truth matters to me in a very intimate way because in understanding philosophy more deeply - in grasping its truth more thoroughly, in other words - the world I inhabit becomes more
personally meaningful. Of course, it is not uncommon to have certain very developed interests and still be driven by gross and habit-
ual self-deception in other important areas of one's life; and when
assessing the self-rule of such a person, we will rightly conclude
that all things considered she is severely deficient in realism. Yet,
in the context of the interests she has developed deeply, she evinces
a profound allegiance to the truth, and a corresponding suppression
of the various ways in which she is apt to evade the claims of
reality. To that extent, these interests make her lapse less grievously from the ideal of realism than she would have without them.
And if her interests were not directed exclusively towards the satisfaction of the social desire, their development would tend to pro-

duce a greater independence of mind. Perhaps, more important, in developing an interest, it is ordinarily true that an individual significantly enlarges her scope for the exercise of autonomy because the accession of understanding entailed will ordinarily increase her freedom to do things she is deeply interested in doing.

If the development of our interests is related to self-rule in the ways I have just suggested, then we have good reason to make the development of children's interests a fundamental concern in schooling. For this is an area where systematic learning under the direction of teachers will clearly be enormously valuable. I may develop my interests somewhat through learning which occurs fortuitously in virtually any social setting, but the deepening of my understanding which that process implies will be greatly enhanced by the resources of the school. The value of these resources are especially salient with respect to enlarging the students' scope to exercise autonomy. The so-called "hidden curriculum" in all sorts of social settings may work powerfully for or against the growth of the autonomous character. Once we acknowledge that autonomous lives do not necessarily revolve around intellectual endeavour, we cannot reasonably say that the school is *the* pivotal institution in shaping autonomous characters. Yet the school surely does have a distinctive contribution in its immense power to make us able, and hence free, where ignorance and the like had previously curtailed the range of our open options. That is precisely the point of the comparison I sketched earlier between the cultured polymath and the unschooled rustic.

But if the development of students' interests is not central to the kind of schooling we provide, then we cannot seriously claim that personal autonomy is central to our conception of education. Consider the alternatives. Suppose we set about teaching children what we believe is good for them, regardless of what effect it has on their interests, or else we give slight attention to the development of their interests while concentrating our efforts elsewhere. In either case we are not treating the fate of Sharon as the educational atrocity which it clearly is. Alternatively, we might turn the school into a place where children merely pursue their interests. But that would be to invite a different kind of failure. If pursuing one's interests does not necessarily produce any substantial learning, an institution devoted to that end could not purport to be centrally concerned with education, much less an education for autonomy.

In order to appreciate what I am recommending, it is crucial to avoid certain conceptual errors which have bedevilled the discussion of child-centred education. It is often vaguely suggested that schooling should be based upon the learner's interests, needs, purposes, desires, and so forth, as if these various terms were virtually interchangeable. In the influential writings of John Dewey, whose capacity to obliterate important distinctions is often truly sublime, such confusions are especially prominent. In his *Democracy and Education*, Dewey conflates aim, intent, end, interest, affection, concern, and motivation in a semantic pot-pourri: differences in "emphasis" are supposed to be the only important distinctions between the first three concepts and the last four. It would be tedious to discuss how interests are to be distinguished from the various things with which they are prone to be confounded, and if a satisfactory analysis of the concept has already been offered, it should be unnecessary. But it must be understood that the demand that care must be taken in interpreting the proposal that we develop children's interests is of the utmost practical importance. Failure in this regard will either discredit the proposal altogether or else thwart attempts to implement it. It is extremely damaging, for example, to misunderstand the connection between our interests and our occurrent desires. What we occurently desire commonly reflects our interests because it is explained by what interests us. However, it is easy to fall into the trap of supposing that the connection is rather closer than this. One might assume that the individual's desires always reflect underlying interests. In that case, letting the child do whatever she desires will mean that she does what interests her; and if an interest-based curriculum is conceived as one that merely facilitates the efforts of children to do what interests them, then we have arrived at an egregiously permissive conception of schooling. The school is doing its proper job when students are doing what they want to do, and the proper role of the "teacher" is just to get out of the way. But even when we avoid these gross conceptual errors, the idea of an interest-based curriculum has still not received the critical attention it deserves, as we shall presently see.

The relevance or irrelevance of children's interests to curriculum planning is not exactly a burning issue among contemporary philosophers of education or policy-makers. I suspect that most educators assume that the matter was settled in the late 1960s, when the child-centred tradition was more influential within the educational establishment than it is today and philosophers of education were anxious to expose its inadequacies. The philosophical literature from this period which addresses the idea of an interest-based curriculum commonly fails to differentiate the various interpretations to which it is open, and the idea of such a curriculum is apt to be rejected on grounds applicable only to the least reasonable interpretations. One can see this clearly in the widely read and highly regarded writings of Dearden, Hirst, and Peters. In *The Philosophy of Primary Education*, Dearden deplores the excessive preoccupation with "starting from children's interests" among adherents of child-centred education, though he commends their success in "searching for and developing more interesting ways of teaching";[4] and in a similar vein, Hirst and Peters claim that the interests of pupils are more relevant to the method of teaching than the content of education.[5] These authors do not entirely discount the possibility that the child's interests should carry some weight, however slight, in determining what she is to learn at school, but they overwhelmingly emphasize the methodological relevance of interest. That is to say, they maintain that once we have decided upon the aims and content of the curriculum, we should adopt methods of teaching which appeal to student's current interests to avoid unnecessary drudgery and encourage the emergence of new and worthwhile interests. There is an important contrast between this position and the one I have been defending. If the development of children's interests should be central to the conduct of schooling, then we cannot only pay serious attention to them when questions about teaching methods are being considered. That concern will ordinarily oblige us to select content with a close eye to our students' interests and to make substantial adjustments in this direction or that according to their ongoing development. If the position taken by Dearden, Hirst, and Peters is to be justified, the arguments marshalled in its support must show that the development of children's interests should not be a vital concern in the determination of educational content. However, the arguments they present do not show this.

First, these authors maintain that the interests children bring to the classroom are the result of social influences which are not always desirable. As Dearden points out, many children grow up in bookless homes where indiscriminate television-watching and the like are the order of the day. "In such circumstances, simply to start from existing interest is to trivialise the curriculum and to give the school's endorsement to interests which may be positively at variance with the purposes of education."[6]

Suppose we accept Dearden's rather grim assessment of the culture of contemporary families. The educational conclusion he draws from that assessment looks pretty rash once we become alert to the ambiguity of "starting from existing interests." If anyone suggested that we start from them just by letting children do whatever they are interested in doing, then Dearden's argument will provide a telling rebuttal. But it will not be relevant at all if we take the position I have advocated about the proper relation between interests and the curriculum. Perhaps many of our students' interests are unacceptable for moral or prudential reasons, and others are so cognitively impoverished that they will not sustain any prolonged development. We should obviously not indulge *these* propensities in the classroom. However, I assume that all the interests of the typical child in our culture are not so unredeemably immoral, imprudent, or trivial that the attempt to develop any of them in depth will lead to a trivial curriculum or the endorsement of anti-educational predilections; and if that very mildly optimistic assumption is correct, then starting from the child's interests (in one sense) will typically be defensible against Dearden's argument.

But what if my assumption is wrong? And even if it is right what is to be done for those untypical children whose existing motivational structures are utterly bereft of educational potential? If a child were in this sorry state, then I suppose we must present her with activities she is currently uninterested in. It does not follow that our concern with developing her interests must be abandoned until some point in the future when she is at last thoroughly civilized. As interest begins to kindle in some of the things she is taught, we will have good reason to adjust curricular content to permit intensive study in those areas; and whatever fails to elicit her interest should be dropped from her curriculum, other things being equal. Whether we frequently or only rarely find children in this sorry state does not affect the point at issue. In neither case would their predicament justify our being any less concerned with developing their interests.

Dearden and others repeatedly claim that the child-centred tradition fails to recognize the teacher's important role in stimulating new interests.[7] This no doubt carries weight against some proposals made by exponents of that tradition, but it does nothing to undermine what I have endorsed. Stimulating an entirely new interest is certainly different from developing some existing one, even though the conceptual boundary between the two is vague. Moreover, if we want autonomy for our children a case can be made for encouraging and perhaps even compelling them to explore novel activities and subjects because, in doing so, they may discover aptitudes they had previously been unaware of, and their concomitant greater self-knowledge will increase their scope for the expression of autonomy. But we must not get these facts out of perspective – a school where teachers are successful in originating new and fruitful interests will certainly be one where students are, for the most part, developing their existing interests.

This claim requires some explanation. Presumably, the new and worthwhile interests Dearden and others want children to acquire will involve, at least eventually, a fairly deep understanding of certain things – music, literature, science, and the like – and this understanding will give them access to a fertile area of intrinsically valued experience and achievement. In other words, schooling is supposed to usher in certain fairly highly developed interests. However, we cannot reasonably expect that outcome unless some interest is engendered early in the process of schooling and subsequently developed through intensive study. It may sometimes happen that a child studies music or literature year after year, driven purely by extrinsic incentives and disincentives; and then, as schooling draws to a close, a developed interest dramatically erupts as a result of long years of drudgery. If that were the ordinary course of events, we could still be confident that schools that did not pay much attention to developing students' existing interests, might be successfully originating new ones. But that is patently not the ordinary course of events.

Finally, it is suggested that we cannot expect everything children need to learn at school to be immediately interesting. At an early age, interests are apt to be sporadic and evanescent, according to Hirst and Peters, and by just following wherever they lead we are liable to instil "a promiscuous attitude towards activities, a tendency to give them up when their initial appeal fades and difficulties are encountered."[8] It must be acknowledged that children may sometimes need to learn at school what does not interest them at all. The extent to which that may justify departures from an interest-based curriculum will not be addressed until the final section of this chapter, when I will examine the importance of some curricular aims other than autonomy. My limited objective here is to assess the weight of the empirical claims about children's interests which Hirst and Peters use to support their thesis about the divergence between interests and educational needs. Again, although these claims may well be true, their being so would not discredit the kind of curriculum I am advocating.

In the process of developing an interest one is often obliged to learn things which have no immediate appeal. If I try to develop my interest in philosophy through a deeper appreciation of contemporary phenomenology and existentialism, I might find that I cannot progress as far as I want without learning German and grappling with the intricacies of certain murky philosophical texts. Although much of this may not be immediately interesting, it might eventually be richly rewarding. Of course, Hirst and Peters point out that this kind of effort will generally not be forthcoming from children – or at least young children – and so their interests will remain primitive unless we intervene. Yet the fact that we may have to intervene sometimes does not mean that we thereby abandon or even curb our attempts to develop their interests. I will grant that if one persistently has to bribe or threaten a child to read Shakespeare, then it is quite clear that one is not developing her interest in drama. If a more developed interest entails finding out more of what is intrinsically valuable in activities appropriate to its object, then it necessarily brings a stronger motive to engage in those activities, other things being equal. For that reason, where extrinsic motives have to be persistently brought into play, development evidently is not taking place. Nevertheless, common psychological states interfere with our doing what would develop our interests – the aversion, emphasized by Hirst and Peters, to what is intellectually taxing, the fear of failure or novelty, and so on. And if these states were more frequent during early childhood, the use of extrinsic incentives or disincentives might be justified fairly often by our desire to develop the child's interests. So there is nothing here to detract from my case.

In fairness to Dearden, Hirst, and Peters, it should be noted that their strictures upon child-centred education were a salutary corrective to many silly claims that have been made under the aegis of that tradition. Indeed, they were rather more careful than Dewey or any of his precursors in trying to discern what an interest-based curriculum would involve. But they were not careful enough.

In arguing against the position on children's interests usually taken by contemporary philosophers of education I have made none of those extravagant assumptions which have been associated with child-centred education. The opaque metaphysical doctrine that children are naturally good lurks nowhere in the previous paragraphs. I do not assume that children are driven by voracious intellectual appetites or that social influences outside the school are generally favourable to education. I do not pretend that personal discovery is the high road to understanding. Furthermore, in presenting an argument for an interest-based curriculum which holds independently of these assumptions, I have not burdened the argument with so many qualifications and caveats that what is recommended becomes barely distinguishable from what usually goes on in schools nowadays or what critics of the child-centred tradition would advocate. I think I am on safe ground in saying that the story of Sharon closely resembles the history of many children in our schools and that contemporary philosophers of education, who have little sympathy for child-centred doctrines, also have little appreciation of the relevance of children's interests to questions of educational content.

The teacher who wants autonomy for her students will be concerned with more than the development of their interests; she will also want these interests to be integrated into a motivational structure which instantiates realism and independence of mind to a high degree. I have suggested that the development of interest will naturally contribute to autonomy, but other practices will obviously contribute to that end as well. For example, children may have to be made vividly aware of the consequences of a decision to develop intensively one particular interest at the expense of others, especially where the consequences will have far-reaching effects upon their future lives. A student might cultivate a particular interest against the background of some fantasy about the self – an illusion about the extent of her talents perhaps – which the teacher has at least a *prima facie* duty to dissipate. But none of this diminishes the need for a kind of schooling that affords ample scope for variation in curricula according to the bent of the individual's interests because we cannot reasonably expect development to take the same, predictable direction for all students. In any event, because an immense variety of possible directions is compatible with the demands of autonomy as a personal ideal, an immense variety of curricula should not bother us so long as our concern is for autonomy as an educational ideal.

This conclusion opens up a fundamental contrast between my own conception of the kind of curriculum fitted for an education for autonomy and the conception J.P. White has elaborated recently. For White, an education for autonomy requires a compulsory curriculum which would severely limit the student's opportunity for specialization according to interest. The arguments that might be developed to support his position are sufficiently weighty to merit very close analysis.

A difficulty in interpreting White's writings is that he nowhere gives more than cursory attention to what he means by "autonomy," even though the curriculum he recommends is supposedly justified by its contribution to autonomy. Perhaps this has something to do with his distaste for the "conceptual joustings" which have occupied philosophers of education over the past couple of decades.[9] However, when a concept is central to an argument and has such shallow roots in ordinary language that a shared understanding cannot be safely assumed, then a bit of conceptual jousting is called for, even if one is anxious to move to more exciting business.

In one passage, however, White appears to be gesturing towards an ideal that might be close to the version of autonomy I have commended. We shall see that there are reasons why someone who is drawn to my concept might also be attracted to White's compulsory curriculum, though I will also show that the appeal of these reasons is ultimately deceptive. In his portrayal of "the educated man," White stresses the priority of dispositions over knowledge, and among the dispositions he specifies are some which are subsumed within the concept of autonomy I have elaborated – independence of mind, courage, prudence, and lucidity.[10] (My emphasis upon resistance to temptation in the regulation of an autonomous will entails that courage and prudence are part of autonomy since each of those virtues is essentially a proneness to resist a certain kind of temptation when framing the will in a spirit of truthfulness. "Lucidity" might be intended to designate something like the suppression of self-deception which I emphasized.) For White, the educated man is the autonomous individual. Therefore, given some of the virtues which constitute his educational ideal, there are some grounds for supposing that his concept of "autonomy" is not much different from mine. For the present I shall assume that no such difference exists. The question then arises as to whether or not White's curriculum really does serve the ideal of character I elaborated in chapter two.

One recurrent theme in White's writings is the idea that ignorance can close off options as effectively as external interference.[11] If I have no understanding of mathematics, then the options of doing geometry or algebra are as ineligible for me as they would be for someone who was mathematically competent but unfree to exercise her skills because of an act of force. The analysis of freedom offered in chapter one would support this point. Moreover, in light of the connection between freedom and autonomy, one can readily agree with White that an education for autonomy will involve an attempt to liberate students from the constraining effect of ignorance upon their options. But that clearly does not help us determine the content of curricula. If the ideal of autonomy is to provide some substantive direction in curriculum development, it must warrant the adoption of some particular kind of curriculum, or at least justify our rejecting some commonly espoused curricula; and the trivial fact that knowledge of some sort should be included (possibly along with other outcomes of learning), does not provide direction of this sort.

In his first book, *Towards a Compulsory Curriculum*, White identified activities which properly belong within a compulsory curriculum largely (though not exclusively) on the basis of a formal subdivision within the broad category of pursuits which presuppose learning of some sort. These can be divided, exhaustively, into two classes, in which: "(1) no understanding of what it is to want X is logically possible without engaging in X; (2) some understanding of what it is to want X is logically possible without engaging in X."[12] It is possible, for example, to acquire some understanding of the desire to play soccer without actually playing the game. Watching others play might suffice or one could obtain enough understanding just by hearing someone explain the rules of the game and extol the pleasures of participation. For that reason soccer belongs to category two (henceforth *C.2*). On the other hand, one could not grasp why someone might want to do mathematics unless one had actually engaged in it. It is certainly possible to explain the point of doing mathematics to someone who knew nothing about it, but the explanation could not succeed unless one were drawn into reflection on such things, for example, as the logical relations between numbers. She would have to *do* some mathematics in order to understand it as a possible object of desire. Therefore, mathematics belongs to category one (henceforth *C.1*), along with science, aesthetic appreciation, philosophy, and communication.

White argues that we must ensure that all our children engage in all *C.1* activities because without such participation they must remain "cut off from all these possible options."[13] Conversely, *C.2* activities may be made available, even if an individual never engages in them. White assumes that a compulsory curriculum at school is necessary to guarantee the requisite level of understanding for *C.1* activities. In addition to what is compulsory, White argues for a voluntary curriculum, comprising a broad range of studies children might want to pursue in depth.[14] Presumably, the students' desires determine what is included here, and it does not matter whether what is studied belongs to *C.1* or not.

The issue of compulsion for the sake of educational ends is difficult and the following chapter will contain a fairly detailed discussion of this matter. For the present I want to emphasize one rather obvious fact. If we are to have educational grounds for compelling someone to learn X rather than Y, then either of the following must be shown to be true: (i) X is more educationally valuable than Y and might not be learnt without compulsion or; (ii) X has educational value and is unlikely to be learnt without compulsion whereas Y, though perhaps even more educationally valuable than X, is likely to be learnt without compulsion. Even if I showed one of these conditions to be satisfied, I could be still far short of a decisive argument for compulsion – arguments against paternalism would still have to be disposed of, for instance. My point is simply that considerations of educational value could give no support whatever to compulsion if neither (i) nor (ii) were true. If White's argument is to carry weight, he must show that the priority he gives to $C.1$ pursuits in the curriculum is defensible along the lines indicated in (i) or (ii).

White does not attempt to justify his compulsory curriculum via (i), and it is hard to see how he could succeed if he tried. He points to no specific feature of $C.1$ activities which would make them more desirable, given that autonomy is our measure of educational value, than others. Indeed, the fact that in one case understanding is only possible through direct participation while in the other it is not, would appear to be quite irrelevant to the question of what will contribute more to self-rule. In order to see if White's argument can survive via (ii), it is necessary to ask just what degree of understanding in each $C.1$ activity students are supposed to achieve before compulsion becomes unwarranted. What he prescribes is "some understanding" of the desire to engage in an activity, but that is vague enough to admit a substantial range of reasonable interpretation.[15] Clearly, the more stringent our criterion of an adequate understanding, the more reason we have to suppose that it is unlikely to be met without compulsion. But if we adopt an even mildly stringent criterion, then the case for *excluding* virtually all $C.2$ activities from the compulsory curriculum collapses entirely. We cannot suppose that children are likely to acquire anything close to a substantial understanding of the desire to engage in each $C.2$ pursuit without compulsory study. After all, when they are not subject to compulsion, children are not obsessively occupied with watching the participants of each $C.2$ activity, listening attentively to the reasons why they participate, or trying out each pursuit to see what it has to offer. Therefore, on anything close to a stringent interpretation of what counts as "some understanding," White cannot justify the priority he assigns to $C.1$ in the curriculum.

If White's argument were to succeed, he would have to accept a less demanding criterion of understanding. But that course would merely create other, and equally forbidding difficulties. I do not think it is plausible to say that without compulsory study children are unlikely to attain even a negligible understanding of the desire to appreciate art, study physics, do mathematics, and so on, but likely to come to understand the point of artistic creation, learning a second language, and the like. But suppose I am wrong about this. If we gave White the benefit of the doubt here, he could defend the priority he gives to $C.1$ along the lines of (ii), so long as he accepted a very lax standard of an adequate understanding. Unfortunately that would be a very hollow victory for White since he could only approve of the compulsory study of $C.1$ pursuits until a paltry level of understanding was attained in each. The compulsory curriculum would shrink almost to a vanishing point. The voluntary curriculum would dominate the child's life at school, which would simply be a matter of learning whatever one wanted to learn or nothing at all if that were one's inclination. In that event, White's conception of the curriculum would be vulnerable to the same criticisms often made against radically permissive versions of child-centred education.

In short, the argument of *Towards a Compulsory Curriculum* posed a dilemma for White. On the one hand, if he adopted anything close to a stringent criterion of an adequate understanding for each activity, he would have to concede that we have just as much reason to include all $C.2$ as all $C.1$ pursuits within the compulsory curriculum. If that were so, then White would have to endorse an alarmingly inclusive compulsory curriculum: children would be compelled to study just about everything until they acquired a substantial understanding of why one might want to do just about anything. The inclusiveness of this curriculum is alarming because the vast extent of the compulsion it requires would seem inimical to the values of freedom and autonomy White is anxious to uphold. Alternatively, he might be able to justify excluding virtually all $C.2$ pursuits from the curriculum if he chose a very weak criterion of understanding. But that position, as we have seen, leads to a minute and trivial compulsory curriculum.

White's subsequent writings do not explicitly note this dilemma, but much of his more recent work can be understood as a way of trying to address it. In his current position, he now appears to advocate a very extensive compulsory curriculum. But we need not be alarmed by its scale, or so he would have us believe. Children may indeed be compelled to engage in or learn about both $C.1$ and $C.2$ activities.[16] Although this entails a massive encroachment upon liberty, that is no reason to reject it, or so White claims, because the principle of liberty – what he means by this is the principle of noninterference – only applies to our dealings with self-determining adults.[17] It is also, at least on the face of it, a feasible curriculum if all the years of compulsory schooling were systematically devoted to its implementation, and other institutions, such as the family, helped in compelling the child to achieve the requisite level of understanding.[18]

White may be on shaky ground in supposing that the principle of liberty is irrelevant to our dealings with children. In chapter four it should become clear that he is. However, if the curriculum he recommends were defensible in terms of autonomy, there would be a strong argument for supposing that the loss of freedom it exacts is a price worth paying. Where particular liberties are sacrificed for the sake of autonomy, there will necessarily be good reason to support that policy if I have been right in maintaining that the value of freedom is largely derived from that of autonomy. For instance, we want freedom of worship for everyone so they can express their autonomy in religious matters, but that, in turn, requires that we sacrifice everyone's freedom to persecute heretics. The sacrifice of freedom implicit in White's extensive compulsory curriculum might be defensible along similar lines. I would suggest that two related aspects of his curriculum might be used to construct such a defence. First, it may be argued that the compulsory curriculum will yield a massive array of options for the learner when compulsory study is completed. That is to say, the temporary loss of freedom endured within the compulsory curriculum will be more than offset by an extensive increase in freedom acquired through the knowledge of various possible objects of desire which compulsion ensures. Second, in exploring a multitude of diverse activities, the child will be absorbed in a quite thorough exploration of her native talents and aptitudes and will therefore be protected against the constraining effects on choice of ignorance about her natural aptitudes. I shall examine each of these points in turn.

The argument I developed earlier about the connection between autonomy and freedom implies that a compulsory curriculum will substantially increase the individual's freedom of choice only if the learning it fosters bears a certain relation to the interests of the individual. The options it provides have to be internal to the expression of interests she already has or could well come to acquire under certain conditions. A compulsory curriculum will not have this liberating effect if it achieves breadth of knowledge only at the expense of developing the child's interests.

Against this, it might be objected that in dealing with younger children, whose interests are prone to be transitory, multifarious and likely to have little connection to what will occupy them as adults, a curriculum devoted to developing their current interests is unlikely to contribute significantly to the freedom they will eventually possess as more or less autonomous adults. If the interests of the adult are apt to be utterly different from those of the child, then a curriculum which maximizes the adult's freedom is apt to have little or no connection to what currently interests the child. It could be inferred from this that we should choose a curriculum which introduces the child to as many different activities as possible, whether they interest her or not, for the sake of the autonomous adult whom we hope she will eventually become.

This counterargument only has any credibility when we are discussing curricula for very young children. Only there does it seem reasonable to assume that a radical discontinuity between the interests of the child and the adult is likely, though it is certainly possible that empirical inquiry would reveal that such discontinuity is rather less frequent than we assume. At any rate, it is obvious that as the child grows older and her motivational structure begins to stabilize, the probability of fundamental changes occurring decreases. The adolescent who finds Shakespeare ineffably boring is hardly likely to become passionately interested once she turns the corner into adulthood. Consequently, the most that the counterargument can establish is that a Whitean compulsory curriculum is desirable for younger children.

But even if the counterargument applies only to the curricula of younger children, it still does not succeed. Suppose we know that the interests of the particular children we are teaching are likely to be utterly different from the interests they will have as adults, and hence, whatever we might do to develop the former is likely to add little to the freedom of the adults they will become in time. We still cannot know what interests they will have as adults, and therefore we cannot know that any alternative to an interest-based curriculum will conduce to greater freedom for the adult. In those circumstances it might appear arbitrary, if indeed autonomy is our standard of educational value, whether we opt for an interest-based curriculum or White's compulsory curriculum. Since we cannot know which curriculum will maximize the adult's freedom, our commitment to autonomy cannot determine which curriculum we should choose. But that is too hasty. For we can still ask which curriculum would respect more the child's *current* level of autonomy.

I take it that even the behaviour of our youngest pupils is normally to be explained in terms of choices on their part rather than inexorable internal drives or external pressures, and, in choosing, they necessarily evince at least a modicum of realism and independent-mindedness. The arguments presented in the previous chapter in support of autonomy are as applicable to children as they are to adults. To be sure, one might argue cogently that we are justified in discounting the agent's current evaluations and choices where we can be sure that such a policy would ensure a transition to a higher level of autonomy. But that is not the kind of case we are considering. What we are faced with are alternatives which we cannot adjudicate between on the basis of long-term consequences for autonomy because we do not know what the consequences will be. In these circumstances, the best policy is the one that shows more respect for the child's current level of autonomy, and an interest-based curriculum is the on to be preferred by that criterion. Such a curriculum does not give students a licence to do whatever they choose in the classroom, but it is systematically based on a regard for the child's evaluations – a regard noticeably absent from White's alternative.

However, one could still claim that a compulsory curriculum of the sort espoused by White would provide greater protection against those constraints upon choice caused by ignorance of native aptitudes. That argument would be especially powerful if the extent of one's autonomy were a function of one's self-knowledge. Although I showed in chapter two that autonomy and self-knowledge are not so closely intertwined, the argument still has some merit even if that tight connection does not hold. Once the development of the child's interests is a central concern in curriculum selection, we can reasonably expect that in many instances learning will take rather specialized directions at an early stage of schooling. After all, it is empirically obvious that the individual's interests will fall into a limited number of quite specific categories. Broad and enduring interest in a vast range of different activities is surely a rare phenomenon. It follows that an interest-based curriculum, in the sense I have recommended, would normally leave the individual ignorant of certain widely prized areas of human endeavour. The artistically-inclined child, say, might end up with little understanding of mathematics or the sciences. Her choice of a life which revolves around the arts may have been a highly autonomous one. Nevertheless, her situation could still parallel that of the unschooled rustic who makes her choices through ignorance of the alternatives. Our hypothetical child could be a latent Einstein. In that case, ignorance of her own scientific talents would make her unfree in a vitally important respect because it would prevent her from choosing the form of life she would find more fulfilling than any other. This is doubtless an extreme case. But when education takes a fairly specialized turn in the early stages, we can certainly expect that interests which might have emerged after a bit more study will never do so, and the lack of self-knowledge which guarantees that outcome will also guarantee a loss of freedom.

The counterargument just presented points to one way in which an interest-based curriculum is likely to curtail the liberty to exercise autonomy which the child achieves through learning. The question we have to face is whether that likelihood gives us enough reason to assign overriding importance to breadth of knowledge in the aims of schooling. I think further reflections shows that it does not. If we look more carefully at the case of the latent Einstein, it becomes apparent that the loss of freedom likely to ensue from the adoption of an interest-based curriculum raises no insuperable difficulty for its defenders. If this child's artistic interests were intensively developed through her curriculum and she autonomously chose a life which revolved around the arts, then her curriculum would indeed be immensely liberating. It would secure for her a range of options pertaining to things she is deeply interested in doing. One can still grant that a different curriculum would have been even more liberating in its effects, but then one is comparing a highly liberating one with an even more liberating curriculum. Therefore, the costs to freedom involved in foregoing the kind of compulsory curriculum White recommends are less than appalling, even in an admittedly extreme case like the present one. Further, the costs to freedom created by White's alternative are rather more daunting. Insofar as we focus the curriculum upon the plethora of things the child is not now interested in to disclose all hidden aptitudes, we have correspondingly less opportunity to foster learning which opens up options by developing the child's present interests. The loss of freedom suffered when we take that course is only offset by very uncertain gains. It is crucial to bear in mind that although we can significantly enhance the child's freedom by ensuring that she has options pertaining to interests she will acquire later on – perhaps when some hidden talent emerges – we are almost completely in the dark about what these will be. Indeed, when our judgments on this matter are not purely speculative, it is because we see some new interest as the likely consequence of the development of some already existing one. It would simply be irrational to abandon the development of the child's present interests for the sake of breadth of learning, if enhancing the freedom to exercise autonomy is our goal. In the former case, we can be sure that our efforts would be substantially liberating once development occurs, whereas in the latter we will inevitably be groping in the dark, hoping that we might unleash the passionate interest in science of an Einstein, and that perhaps most students would acquire some interest in subjects they would otherwise have shunned entirely. But these unpredictable and fitful successes, liberating though they would be, have to be weighed against the very serious loss of freedom resulting from a failure to develop the child's existing interests.

I am certainly willing to concede that the possibility of discovering hidden aptitudes and kindling new passions will sometimes justify brief incursions into currently uninteresting activities. My point is simply that if we are concerned with making our children more autonomous and enlarging the freedom they have to exercise autonomy, then we should not give priority to breadth of learning over the development of their interests.

Even if this conclusion holds, one may still doubt that I have done justice to White's position. I have assumed that what White and I mean by "autonomy" is quite similar, but that could well be false. Consider the following pivotal move in *The Aims of Education Restated*:

It is a popular thesis of contemporary philosophy that the individual's good consists in the satisfaction of those desires which, on *reflection*, he prefers to be satisfied, given a full understanding of all possible options. Educationally, this generates the aim of equipping the pupil to work out what he most prefers to do, e.g., by providing him with an understanding of different ends-in-themselves and seeing that he develops the disposition to make reflective and therefore autonomous choices.[19]

In this passage, choosing reflectively, or at least choosing where reflection is informed by an understanding of different ends-in-themselves, is assumed to be sufficient for autonomous choice; and it is clear that what White has in mind is strongly autonomous choice and not the minimal autonomy presupposed by any instance of choosing. But the bare concept of *reflective* choice, even if we stipulate that it must include an understanding of different ends-in-themselves, is not tightly connected to autonomy in the sense that we have been concerned with so far. It is altogether possible that I could choose after reflection and with "a full understanding of all possible options" and yet my choice would indicate a striking lapse from independence of mind. A strong disposition to choose reflectively might also betoken a serious lack of realism if it were rooted, say, in self-deception about one's own need for spontaneity in personal relationships; and that failure could even coincide with a polymathic understanding of different ends-in-themselves. The conflation of autonomy with post-reflective choice is by no means rare in White's work,[20] and it clearly lends itself to a rather different interpretation of his position than the one I have been pursuing. Perhaps the curriculum he recommends is well designed to foster autonomy in a different sense from mine. However, I hope to show that although White's curriculum is well designed to serve autonomy as post-reflective choice, he provides no viable argument for favouring that particular ideal. In fact, further scrutiny will show that it is unattractive as an educational ideal for all persons.

It is easy to see why identifying the individual's autonomy (and her good) with postreflective choice would lead to a curriculum of the sort White has championed. In fact, the realization of autonomy would be logically impossible without such a curriculum once the necessary reflection is taken to entail a knowledge of all possible options. And the misgivings I have expressed about White's prescriptions would be entirely unwarranted if postreflective choice ought to be our central concern. Since the individual's good is to be found only in interests and desires which are approved after informed reflection, policies which run completely against the grain of prereflective desires and interests do not adversely affect the individual's good at all. A massive compulsory curriculum designed to facilitate informed reflection should not trouble us, even if it were wholly uninteresting for all its recipients, because it would not interfere with the good of its recipients.

This line of interpretation might seem inappropriate because White does sometimes speak of the "postreflective-desire-satisfaction theory of the good" as if it required us to locate the good (and hence autonomy) in a *via media* between reflection and commitment to our projects.[21] But this is to endorse a *different* theory of the good and therefore a different version of autonomy. If one believes that "the individual's good consists in the satisfaction of those desires which, on *reflection*, he prefers to be satisfied, given a full understanding of all possible options," then the good has yet to be determined for anyone who lacks a full understanding of all options. Commitment to one's projects only becomes relevant to the good after the necessary understanding is attained. At any rate, White's curricular recommendations are much more reasonably viewed as serving the value of postreflective choice than the kind of *via media* to which he sometimes alludes. For the compulsory component of the curriculum he envisions, with its emphasis on vast breadth and little depth of knowledge, clearly has little or nothing to do with enhancing commitment to one's projects; and the voluntary curriculum will enhance commitment only if students decide to use it with that end in view. In seems a bit reckless to assume that all or even most students will decide to use it in that way.

Chapter two examined White's argument that autonomy was desirable by virtue of (the alleged) unavailability of moral expertise, and I tried to show that the argument was unsound. Does it look any better when construed as a defense of postreflective choice rather than autonomy in the sense I have elucidated? I do not think it does. One can only abandon the concept of ethical expertise by maintaining that we cannot know when someone is better situated than someone else to answer questions of value. The rejection of ethical expertise carries with it a radical and very implausible scepticism about the application of reason to such questions, and it is a scepticism which is as repugnant to the ethical ideal of postreflective choice as it is to any other. For it implies that we cannot know whether teachers who compel students to set aside prereflective desires for the sake of postreflective choice are any better situated to discern their students' good than the students themselves.

Although postreflective choice cannot be justified through the epistemological defense White sketches, it could be an appealing ideal for all that. But I think whatever appeal it has depends on confusing autonomy (in my sense) with postreflective choice; and once we have sorted out those two concepts, it becomes clear that the pursuit of the latter as an educational ideal for all would threaten the cultivation of autonomy. To the extent that we have good reason to cultivate autonomy, we also have good reason to reject educational ideals with which it conflicts, at least in the absence of further supporting arguments in favour of the rival ideal.

According to White, an education which equips one with a reflective disposition and an understanding of different ends-in-themselves makes one "the final arbiter of his own good, not a blind follower of the authority of others, whether God or men."[22] One can agree that his counts in favour of White's position only if one maintains that individuals should be the final arbiters of their own good. I am not entirely clear what White means by making the individual "the final arbiter" of the good. But there are reasons why those who prize autonomy would want to argue that the good of the individual is highly contingent upon her own choices. Therefore, White's argument may look rather alluring at this point, even if its meaning is not pellucid.

I have argued that a life in which autonomy flourishes is one where the individual possesses a character of a certain kind – she is highly realistic and independent-minded – and used her ample freedom to express her autonomy. It follows that it is only through her own choices that autonomy can thrive. Further, the range of freedom such as individual enjoys affords the possibility of embracing any of myriad forms of life. If we think of the agent's own particular good in light of the ideal of autonomy, it will be the particular life she chooses when she does so in a highly realistic and independent-minded fashion.

An individual could be equipped through education with a thorough knowledge of all ends-in-themselves, as well as a reflective disposition, and still not be psychologically ready to determine her own good through choice in the manner I have just indicated. Suppose Helen makes it clear to her daughter from an early age that unless she always conforms to her mother's religious beliefs she will lose her mother's love. At the same time, Helen insists that her child must learn about all ends-in-themselves, and she encourages the development of a reflective disposition in her daughter which will endure into adulthood. When Helen's daughter reaches adulthood her postreflective choice is to adhere to her mother's faith, but only because she fears, perhaps unconsciously, the loss of her love. White would apparently have us believe that despite Helen's emotional blackmail, she had nonetheless put her child in a situation where she was the "final arbiter" of her own good. Now there may be some sense in which this is true, but for those concerned with self-determination of the good, rooted in the ideal of autonomy, there will be compelling reasons to condemn such an upbringing.

I am sure that White would discount this counterexample. In the circumstances I have described, Helen's daughter would be blindly following the authority of another, and therefore would not be engaged in the *kind* of reflection intrinsic to genuine autonomy. But if we are to stipulate that a reflective disposition precludes the "blind following" which is at odds with realism and independence of mind, then we return to autonomy as it was elucidated in chapter two, and White's position becomes open to my earlier criticisms.

Further, it is crucial to bear in mind that lives characterized by a high degree of reflection are not the only ones compatible with autonomy, in my sense. In forsaking academe for rural simplicity, one may abandon sustained reflection, but not necessarily realism and independence of mind. If we are to follow White's advice and encourage students to maintain reflectiveness as a central feature of their lives, we are to that extent deflecting serious attention from existential options which are not at variance with realism and independence of mind – or with the claims of morality for that matter. In doing so, we reduce the eligibility of these options for all students. For those who by their nature and interests are suited for a life without pervasive reflection, this loss may be severe. If there were some persuasive argument in favour of reflectiveness as an ideal for all persons, then the sacrifice of autonomy to attain this end could well be justifiable. But White certainly provides no such argument and neither does anyone else, as far as I know.

I have tried to show that the kind of schooling which takes personal autonomy as its governing ideal is one that is centrally concerned with developing students' interests. The possibility remains that the school should pursue other educational aims, albeit only as peripheral concerns in the planning of curricula. This should not trouble us unless we were convinced that autonomy was all that mattered in education, and there is no reason to be convinced of this. But another, more unsettling possibility remains. If we examined these rival educational aims and the implications of pursuing them, it might turn out that one or the other should be our paramount concern and the development of children's interests be relegated to a merely peripheral status. An exhaustive exploration of this possibility would carry us very far away from the main lines of my argument. But I think I can allay the most serious qualms about an interest-based curriculum likely to arise here. These qualms revolve around the idea that the interest-based curriculum will not adequately promote the moral education of students.

The degree of success one has by the standards of morality partly depends on how well one understands the good of others, and it has been argued that depth of understanding in this connection cannot be acquired without knowledge of the diverse activities which the good of others may involved. "Now suppose a pupil does not know anything like the whole range of possible options: suppose, in particular, he knows nothing about aesthetic activities. Not only are his options narrowed: his capacity for moral action is also restricted. If he has to vote, for instance, on whether the state should subsidize an opera-house, he cannot fully enter into the point of view of the opera-lover."[23] But right action on the voter's part does not require that he fully enter into the opera-lover's viewpoint. The morally relevant ground for favouring a state subsidy is that the new opera-house would enhance the lives of many people, and presumably, without the subsidy, it would never be built. A thorough appreciation of these grounds is necessary if the voter is to act rightly, but a thorough appreciation is also compatible with knowing virtually nothing of what opera actually is. In fact, this kind of situation is altogether familiar. We are often capable of behaving appropriately to others because we can appreciate the significance of some cherished pursuit in their lives, even though we do not really understand the nature or point of the pursuit. If my wife had only the vaguest ideas about what philosophy is, she could still have a very keen understanding of its significance in my life, and she could show due regard for my need to engage in philosophical activity. If her ideas about philosophy turned out to be entirely mistaken, she would have no understanding of the subject at all, though I cannot see how that would warrant the inference that she could not respect my interest in philosophy.

The understanding of the good of others which moral excellence requires does not imply an understanding of the immense range of activities their good may involve. What children really need to learn here is that the good of others may depend on projects and loyalties which one need *not* understand in order to respect. A curriculum founded on the assumption that there cannot be due respect without understanding will naturally beget the illusion that, for example, if one finds some religion unintelligible, then one should not (because one cannot) recognize its contribution to the good of its adherents. I do not know what would be the most effective method of teaching children that they need not understand an activity in order to acknowledge its value in others' lives. Nevertheless, it is hardly reasonable to suppose that the most effective method would oblige us to relegate the development of children's interests to the status of a marginal concern in curriculum planning.

In another way, however, moral excellence, at least in our present social context, could appear to impost quite taxing cognitive demands upon us. Our recent history has brought into the centre of public controversy certain intellectually formidable moral problems which did not exist previously; it has also revealed the considerable complexity of problems which have existed for a long time but were not deeply understood. A morally admirable person of the nineteenth century did not have to worry about the ethics of nuclear deterrence, genetic engineering, or environmental degradation, and if her beliefs about sexual morality were founded on an unflinching loyalty to tradition, she could hardly be faulted for that. But one might hesitate to describe a person as morally exemplary in current circumstances if she persistently evaded these intellectual intricacies of the moral life. We need more than knowledge and sophisticated reasoning to secure right action, but our need for these does tend to loom especially large nowadays. Therefore, it can be argued that we have to equip each student with the extensive cognitive abilities which an adequate moral education now requires. Perhaps the school is the most effective vehicle for this purpose. If this is true, moral education must surely take precedence over the development of children's interests. I think this is the strongest argument that can be adduced against the idea of an interest-based curriculum, but the challenge it poses can nonetheless be met.

If the relevant question here is which curriculum has the best moral consequences, it is less than obvious that the interest-based variety I have advocated is to be rejected. I assume that the point of morality is to minister in various ways to our having better or more meaningful lives. If it did not matter that human beings can be treated in ways which make their lives better or worse, it would not matter that human beings are capable of vice and virtue. So a curriculum which helps children to develop their interests will, given the value of autonomy, have morally laudable consequences. But it could still be objected that by pushing the development of children's interests to the periphery of teachers' concerns we do not necessarily (and perhaps not even normally) put any very serious obstacle in the way of the development of interests. After all, the process can proceed outside the school, and if we have teachers with a talent for arousing interest in their subject-matter, the development of interests will often be advanced by what happens in the classroom. Of course, parallel and perhaps equally plausible points can be made about the effects of an interest-based curriculum on the acquisition of knowledge and skills relevant to the more intellectually taxing aspects of morality. It can be argued that a good deal of such knowledge and skill will naturally be obtained outside the school, and that much will also be acquired in the classroom whenever students are interested in moral controversies and teachers are capable of developing that interest in appropriate ways. At this point we would appear to have reached a stalemate: each kind of curriculum accords supreme importance to certain morally desirable outcomes while inhibiting (to an extent which is unclear) the achievement of the outcomes favoured by the exponents of the other.

One way of trying to break this stalemate would be to claim that the body of academic accomplishments relevant to the more intellectually sophisticated aspects of the moral life is so vitally relevant that any inhibiting effects on its acquisition might be disastrous. In his trenchant essay, "Education for Survival," Michael Scriven argues for a curriculum of considerable breadth and depth if we are to endure as a morally worthy society.[24] The word "survival" in the title is clearly intended to emphasize the urgency of what is supposed to be at stake. If we fail to give all our students the extensive cognitive equipment for coping with decisions about disarmament and the like, we make it more likely that certain moral disasters will befall us or them in the future. Scriven hopes that his curriculum will engage the interests of students, but I think he would say that if it fails to do so then so much the worse for students' interests. The prospect of a world where people are deeply absorbed in the pursuits and projects which give shape to their lives may be a very attractive one, and an interest-based curriculum promises to contribute to its realization. But there may be no world worth living in at all if our children are not ready to meet the issues with which Scriven and others are preoccupied.

Scriven's position depends on a false picture of what children need to learn in order to cope with intellectually sophisticated moral problems. He would have us believe that what is needed is familiarity with those portions of the academic disciplines which bear upon such problems. I would agree that moral agents in our society must have access to this knowledge if they are to choose wisely. But a curriculum which ensures acquaintance with the relevant knowledge is not the only way of securing access to this knowledge. Another way is rather more likely to ensure the effective utilization of such knowledge.

In some situations, access to knowledge of a certain kind is vital to our well-being, although we may make no attempt to master it ourselves. Instead, we avail of the expertise of others. If I am ill, the treatment I choose will be the one prescribed by a reputable physician; if I am threatened with litigation, the course of action I take will be the one recommended by my lawyer. However, one does have to tread carefully when relying on the expertise of others. At times it is wise to inquire about the qualifications of the putative expert, occasions when a second opinion is called for, and so forth. At any rate, it is clear that foregoing the help of experts in our legal or medical crises is unwise in the ordinary course of events. Given the possibility of using the expertise of others, I would argue that we have as little reason to choose a curriculum comprising a vast body of morally relevant knowledge as we have to choose one comprising a vast body of medical and legal knowledge.

Many would argue that there is a crucial difference between

moral problems and medical or legal problems because, in the latter cases, we have expertise, but not in the former, or so they would claim. I have already suggested that the rejection of ethical expertise is implausible. But even if one could make a cogent argument to justify the move, it certainly could not succeed in a way that debunked expertise in all areas of morally relevant knowledge, such as economics, history, and the other social sciences. We do find our fair share of charlatans in these subjects (as we do in medicine and law). But it is plainly false that no one knows more about economics, say, than anyone else. And if there were no experts here, then what would we include in the curriculum under the rubric of morally relevant economics? If anyone's views about economics are as good or bad as anyone else's, then arguing that economics should be in the curriculum makes as little sense as arguing that the history of the twenty-first century should be included.

A somewhat more promising line of attack would stress the fact that controversy is often rife in areas of knowledge which have moral import, and because the experts disagree, we have to sort things out for ourselves. For example, moral problems about distributive justice are deeply entangled with assumptions about the effects of competing economic policies, and eminent economists disagree vehemently about these assumptions. One might infer that in such circumstances each moral agent must decide for herself which of the rival economic theories is best, and a curriculum which enables her to approximate economic expertise on the relevant issues would achieve that end.

In order to see what is wrong with this, it is useful to press the analogy with medical expertise a bit further. If I were seriously ill and received opposing prescriptions for treatment from two equally distinguished physicians, it would not occur to me to embark on an independent program of medical research about my illness, nor would I be suddenly inspired to enrol in medical school. I might not consider these options simply because I have to decide upon an appropriate treatment *now*. But that is not necessarily the only reason. Suppose a decision about treatment could be delayed for a very long time. It would not make sense to try to become an expert myself unless I had grounds for believing my efforts would make my judgment better than that of any physician I had consulted or could consult. Only then could I maintain that I am better placed to choose correctly than when I have only the discordant prescriptions of other experts to rely upon. By providing children with a curriculum which draws upon the morally relevant bits of the disciplines, we will not equip them to take sides on this or that intellectual controversy with greater assurance of being right than existing experts have. Therefore, a curriculum of this kind cannot be justified by the fact that experts in the morally relevant disciplines so often disagree.

I do not deny that moral problems are especially troubling when experts disagree on possible solutions. My point is simply that the problems are not made any less troubling by attempting to equip students to take sides in these various scholarly disputes. Indeed, such a policy is likely to be damaging in many instances and not just futile. In the context of academic subjects, it is often desirable that experts entertain and defend contradictory theories. Prolonged friction between rival camps, or the shock to orthodox opinion caused by some speculative new theory are potent nutrients in the growth of knowledge. But when a nonexpert addresses an intellectual controversy in which a moral problem is rooted, it is undesirable that she do so in the combative and adventurous spirit we might admire in a scholar. It is imperative that the nonexpert be cautious in the stand she takes because of the importance of what is at issue. Relying on the judgement of any one academic faction may be disastrous since in all likelihood their view will be mistaken. The sensible thing to do is to choose a policy which minimizes the risk of damaging consequences, given the assumption that any of a range of expert opinions might be correct. In order to make that choice, one need not know the evidence adduced in support of each opinion, nor is it necessary to understand each beyond a very superficial level.

The task of enabling students to make effective use of the expertise of others is very important. Perhaps schools have a role in prosecuting that task, and the knowledge and skills which have to be learnt should be taught irrespective of whether students are interested or not. I do not deny any of this. I would merely stress that the task is not so intellectually demanding that it could justify a curriculum devoted to the transmission of morally relevant knowledge with only marginal attention to the development of children's interests.

CHAPTER FOUR

Freedom and Schooling

I have argued that curricula of a certain kind are desirable because of the contribution they would make to self-rule. It does not follow that we have enough reason to compel children to submit themselves to such curricula. It is one thing to establish that some policy or other is desirable, and quite another to show that it should be implemented regardless of the desires of its intended beneficiaries. And if we knew that compulsion were warranted, we would still have to ask about the extent to which it is warranted. It might turn out that compulsory schooling for a few years in childhood is readily justified, while the legitimacy of its extension into adolescence is highly dubious.

But before these two problems can be profitably confronted a number of errors likely to hinder the finding of solutions have to be exposed. Questions about the merits of compulsory schooling came to the fore in educational theory during the 1970s, in large part because of the very controversial work of Ivan Illich and the other deschoolers.[1] Their work is the focus of the opening section of this chapter. Although the deschoolers do not offer anything like satisfactory solutions in the problems of compulsion, by examining the weaknesses of their argument we will be led to a more profound understanding of concepts deeply relevant to the theme of the present chapter. Second, a good deal of liberal hand-wringing about compulsory schooling has recently been inspired by the recognition that the practice is paternalistic, in a certain sense, and therefore fits badly with the traditional liberal aversion to paternalism.[2] I shall argue that the hand-wringing is uncalled for. This will pave the way for the defence of compulsory schooling presented in the final section of this chapter.

Interpreted literally, the demand that we deschool society is the demand that we eradicate schooling. The opaque rhetoric used by Illich and his disciples often makes it difficult to see just what they are espousing, though certain passages in their writings support a literal reading. If we should have no schools at all, then the argument of chapter three is completely undermined and we should certainly have no *compulsory* schooling. The case for deschooling is especially interesting from my viewpoint since much of it hinges on claims about the injurious effects of the school upon personal autonomy.

Yet on other occasions the deschoolers appear to be taking a somewhat less drastic approach to our alleged educational ills. They have frequently urged that we disestablish school, and by this they mean a process parallel to the disestablishment of an official religion. To disestablish a religion is not to eradicate that religion; it is merely to divest it of any favoured status in law or in other state-controlled institutions. The decisive step in disestablishing the school is to do away with compulsory attendance because that is what ensures its privileged status over alternative avenues for learning. But the end of compulsion need not signal the demise of schooling. Schools could well continue to thrive (as disestablished religions have sometimes thrived) when attendance is purely at the discretion of their clients. So two distinct ideas must be disentangled here: the demand that we deschool and the proposal that we merely disestablish school. I shall examine the demand for deschooling first.

There is a crucial distinction between the concept of schooling, with the vast range of possible and actual social practices it encompasses, and the particular varieties of schooling we are familiar with nowadays. The distinction is crucial because if we want to eliminate undesirable features of contemporary schools and assume, incorrectly, that these are essential to the very concept of schooling, we will naturally decide to eliminate the institution altogether, though reflection would show that what is really needed is a better version of the same social practice. There are some grounds for supposing that this confusion underlies many claims made in defence of deschooling. Illich directs much of invective, for example, at aspects of our current educational practices which obviously bear no *conceptual* connection to schooling. He inveighs against the tendency to transform knowledge into an impersonal commodity rather than a personally meaningful acquisition, the debasement of educational achievement through certain procedures of assessment and certification, and the use of such procedures to legitimate economic and political elites.[3] These criticism may or may not be well taken, but even if they are, one wants to know why they warrant deschooling rather than the reform of schools or, indeed, the reform or elimination of other institutions which may cause schools to function in these deleterious ways.

One answer to this question has some initial plausibility. It might be conceded that many of the putative evils of schooling are only contingently connected to the institution. However, these evils have proved remarkably durable in whatever social context the school is placed, sometimes despite serious efforts to extirpate them. The intractability of the contingent evils of schooling gives us reason to do away with the institution rather than attempt a further set of reforms. Several objections to this deserve to be explored. It is by no means obvious that the contingent evils of schooling are as ubiquitous (or even as iniquitous) as Illich assumes; it is even less obvious that we have tried the path of reform with so much seriousness, tenacity, and imagination that our failures reveal the futility of all reform. To develop these points thoroughly one would need far more expertise in social science and history than I can muster. But there is another line of attack against the deschoolers I want to pursue: they direct some of their strictures against the very idea of schooling. These strictures derive much of their appeal from conceptual confusion. More important, by exploring the deficiencies of the deschoolers' arguments in this area, it becomes apparent that one necessarily forfeits educational advantages in deschooling. The weight of these advantages is such that doing away with schools cannot reasonably be commended as a sane, much less a desirable policy. In order to pursue my line of attack, the concept of schooling has to be examined more closely.

Some requirements of schooling are obvious enough to be dealt with very briefly. There must be an institutional setting with the primary purpose of fostering learning of some kind, and the learning must be largely controlled through teaching. The former requirement differentiates schools from families, factories, and so forth; the latter distinguishes schools from academic book clubs, research institutes, poetry appreciation groups, and the like. The concept becomes a bit more troubling if we ask if any other features are essential to its application.

Consider the remarkable work of Paulo Freire in teaching reading to Brazilian peasants while striving to enlarge their political understanding.[4] Freire developed a rather self-effacing style of pedagogy which involved limited explicit direction from the teacher and drew heavily on the limited experience and knowledge of the learner. It is not surprising that his work was halted by the authorities, who were quick to see its subversive potential. So long as Freire was teaching, however, he was not working within the confines of Brazilian schools. Now this might be true only in the sense that Freire operated outside the framework of the Brazilian educational establishment. But suppose his work did not meet an untimely end and had flourished and stabilized as an accepted social practice. Would the resulting practice be recognizable as schooling? I am inclined to think that it would not. My reasons for saying this will become clear if we probe the connection between teaching, authority, and schooling.

R.F. Dearden has argued that in order to teach it is necessary to possess a certain kind of authority over the learner. It is not that the teacher must be *in* authority when she teaches, according to Dearden. She does not have to be "formally recognized to keep order, to direct the movements of pupils, to give or withhold various permissions, to administer punishment should that become necessary, and so on."[5] These policing functions could conceivably be divorced from the task of teaching, though in the world as we know it the policing and the teaching go together. Dearden's point is that the teacher necessarily has authority with respect to activities which are *internal* to the process of teaching, and policing is merely concerned with establishing social conditions which facilitate that process. "The authority necessary to teaching, then, is manifest in such activities as the following: setting tasks, pointing out needs, correcting errors, making critical judgments, identifying dangers and pitfalls, specifying what to do next, directing attention and interest and asking for sample performances."[6] Teachers have the authority to do such things by virtue of their right to structure "the learning situation" and the learner's correlative obligation to comply. If this were true it would be wrong to say, as Dearden does, that the teacher is not necessarily in authority. It would merely be the case that the field of authority intrinsic to teaching does not include the business of policing. For what is essential to being in authority is having an institutional right to direct the conduct of another within some specified field of activity, and that is precisely what Dearden claims teachers necessarily have.

What does it mean to have such a right? In innumerable situations we submit to the direction of others – friends, lawyers, physicians, and so on – without their having any authority to direct us. Of course, our submission could be explained or justified by the fact that the other is seen as *an* authority, but this "epistemic authority" is merely another label for expertise and is only loosely analogous to being in authority. It is well to remember that traffic wardens, school principals, and so forth, need not have any expertise, and one who accepts an obligation to obey them may take a very dim view of their relevant skills and knowledge. Submission to another's direction becomes compliance to authority in the relevant sense only under certain conditions. Those who comply must acknowledge that they have at least a *prima facie* reason to do so because their role makes them subservient in certain respects to the other; those who direct must acknowledge that their role is constituted by rules which entail this reason for compliance on the part of the others. Since a reason for compliance (though not necessarily an overriding reason) is acknowledged simply by virtue of a certain role relationship, the reason will apply even when the direction is seen as ill-advised or otherwise unacceptable. In playing tennis, for example, I would be tacitly rejecting the authority of the umpire if I did not recognize that I had reason to accept her judgments just because she is the umpire. If I accepted them only because I did not want to hurt her feelings, say, or thought her judgments were invariably sound, that would not be enough. In that event, my submission would be indistinguishable from acceptance of nonauthoritative direction.

But there is no reason to suppose that teaching is logically tied to *any* particular field of authority. I will grant that if I am to teach my students they must at least allow me to direct their learning. They must see me as someone a bit more knowledgeable and skilled than they are about what is to be learnt, even though, in fact, I might be an utter charlatan. As a result of this perceived disparity, they might decide to follow my direction on some occasions even when they fail to see its immediate point. Yet all this is a far cry from saying that I must have the right to exercise direction and they must have the obligation to follow. It is hardly doubtful that the sort of thing Freire did in Brazil was teaching, but it is obvious that the relationship he established between teacher and student was not structured around the rights and obligations specified by Dearden. It would be contrary to the spirit of Freirean pedagogy to institute a relationship where students believed they had reason to obey the teacher's commands, say, even when they thought them to be ill-advised.

Dearden's attempt to find a conceptual link between teaching and authority fails; but it may help to explain why one might be reluctant to describe Freirean pedagogy as *schooling*, even in circumstances where it had become a firmly established institution. Perhaps we are willing to apply the word "schooling" only to situations where teaching is practised as a matter of institutional right and students must meet correlative obligations. Other examples come to mind which support that hypothesis. It would be very odd to describe Socrates's fluid entourage of philosophical disciples, dilettantes, and dialectical adversaries as a school, despite the fact that he was, above all else, a teacher for those who joined his circle. The oddness surely has to do with the absence of any pedagogical rights and student obligations. On the other hand, it does seem fitting to speak of the school which Plato created after the death of Socrates. Plato's Academy is not well documented, but the fact that he could designate a successor in his will, for instance, strongly suggests an institution with firmly established rights and obligations of the relevant kind.

These considerations warrant a definition of school along the following lines: an institution is a school if and only if its primary purpose is to foster learning of some kind, the learning is largely directed through the enterprise of teaching, and finally, those who teach have a right to direct the learning of students and students have a corresponding obligation to comply.

The demand that we deschool is the demand that we do away with any institution which meets all the conditions specified in this definition. In particular, two of these conditions have provoked the opposition of the deschoolers. They vehemently object to the way in which teaching controls learning in schools, whatever particular form the school might take, and their anarchistic leanings make them averse to the authority which buttresses pedagogical direction. In their view, schooling militates against our autonomy; it renders us psychologically impotent because we become mindlessly dependent on certified experts and authorities to give direction to our lives. The student supposedly learns that her educational needs cannot be met outside the "client/expert subject/ruler relationship" of student and teacher, and the mental obeisance thereby induced makes her an easy prey for the other oppressive institutions she will soon encounter.[7] In the same vein, Ian Lister claims that because schools teach us that "other people" - viz., the experts and those in authority - should make all the decisions, the schooled individual effectively loses control over her own life.[8] This is an argument about the effects of going to school and for that reason its assessment ultimately depends upon empirical considerations. However, I strongly suspect that the argument's persuasiveness is going to depend in large part on conceptual blunders, and when the blunders have been exposed, we are unlikely to be in serious doubt about where the truth lies.

I suggested earlier, in passing, that in order to teach, the other must see me as being at least a bit more knowledgeable or skilled than herself about what I am trying to teach. Unless I am seen in that light I cannot direct the *learning* of the other, even though I might go through the motions of direction and the other might feign acquiescence. If I attempt to teach history and my students are convinced that I am making up stories as I go along, then so long as their conviction persists, I cannot teach them history. Teaching presupposes that the student defer to the teacher's judgment with regard to the material being taught, and since learning is necessarily directed through teaching in the school, it follows that this attitude will be a pervasive feature of students' participation in any form of that institution. The necessity for this pervasive attitude lends some plausibility to the deschoolers' claims about the psychological impotence any form of schooling is liable to induce.

But the necessity for deference only appears to support the deschooler's position so long as we are unclear about the sense in which deference is required. Suppose I am to teach someone. It is patently not necessary that the other abrogate all independent judgment on the subject I am teaching. What is required is a presumptive deference which is properly withdrawn insofar as teaching is successful. In being taught philosophy, say, one will gradually learn to distinguish good and bad arguments with little external help, one becomes able to decide what is worth reading in the contemporary literature, and so on; and along with this burgeoning critical capacity, the pronouncements of one's teachers, which ignorance initially obliged one to accept on trust, will naturally come under sharper scrutiny. The need to defer to another's judgment is reduced as the original disparity in knowledge between teacher and learner diminishes, giving way to a relationship of approximate intellectual equality. In fact, even at the outset of the relationship between student and teacher it is surely possible and desirable to encourage a deference tempered by a strong sense of the teacher's fallibility.

If teaching demanded a wholly uncritical submission to the teacher's direction, then the deschoolers' argument would be telling. Although submission of that kind might occasionally be desirable or unavoidable, its cultivation as a pervasive attitude in the school would certainly endanger autonomy. But teaching and hence schooling do not require uncritical submission, and it is fantastic to suppose that the deference they do demand would inevitably degenerate into uncritical submission. That supposition is not even compatible with the deschoolers' admiration of Freire's work or their acknowledgment that teaching would have some role in the alternatives to schooling that they favour.[9]

Furthermore, if we abolished all social settings in which learning was systematically directed through teaching, we would forfeit means which are virtually essential to the realization of all but the most unambitious and impoverished conceptions of education. The knowledge and skill we need to acquire in order to take control of our own lives is almost invariably too formidable an achievement for the independent or cooperative efforts of the ignorant. And once we create educational institutions where learning is systematically directed through teaching, we are at least very close to having schools.

But these institutions could conceivably function without anything in the way of pedagogical rights and student obligations. We could create social settings in which knowledgeable and skilled persons direct the learning of those who are relatively ignorant and unskilled without any attendant rights to direct and obligations to acquiesce. That is precisely what Freire and Socrates did. The deschoolers might argue that it is the installation of these rights and obligations in schooling which pose the real threat to autonomy. Where they have not been installed, the student is not deterred from resisting pedagogical direction whenever she comes to see it as unjustified. But once the teacher is in authority, one is obliged to comply, even when the direction is seen as utterly pointless. In other words, because the authority which schooling confers upon teachers means that students must set aside independent judgment, it can be expected that prolonged attendance would inculcate habits of uncritical conformity repugnant to autonomy.

This conclusion loses its appeal once we are sensitive to the difference between a *prima facie* and an absolute obligation to adhere to authoritative direction. An individual only sets independent judgment aside when she accepts an absolute obligation to comply to authority. This would occur if she were led to believe that she could never have a good enough reason to resist. In all circumstances short of that extreme situation, the subjects of authority, whether in the school or elsewhere, face the problem of whether or not their obligation to comply outweighs all considerations that would support a different course of action. The concept of schooling certainly entails no absolute obligations for students to comply with authority.

Furthermore, there are two rather prosaic but nonetheless note-worthy advantages to imposing *prima facie* obligations of compliance upon students. Once there is a substantial difference between teacher and student in their understanding of what is to be taught, it can be expected that fairly often the teacher will want to make an educationally appropriate move which the student is simply incapable of seeing as such. A teacher of philosophy wants students to give serious attention to arguments which appear outrageous to common sense, and so they are naturally inclined to resist her direction. A piano teacher wants a certain piece played slowly and delicately while the student, who has yet to see the value of subtleties in interpretation, is intent on playing everything as fast as possible. It is frequently possible and sometimes desirable for the teacher to stop and explain the point of her direction, but to attempt that *whenever* this impasse is reached for *any* student could impede the progress of teaching to a degree that would be extremely frustrating for all concerned. This gives us reason to create a rule where students are ordinarily expected to acquiesce to pedagogical direction, even when they fail to see its rationale. Instituting that rule would be tantamount to putting the teacher in authority within the sphere of teaching. Another line of reasoning converges towards the same conclusion. In any cooperative endeavour there is the problem of coordinating the efforts of participants in prosecuting their shared purpose. Where many pitfalls stand in the way of success and the contributions of many different persons have to be harmonized, the problem of coordination can hardly be resolved without investing some individual or group with the right to orchestrate the actions of each. Where teaching is a cooperative venture of this kind, the problem of coordination furnishes a powerful reason for bestowing the authority to teach upon teachers.

There are a couple of limitations I would like to point out about the educational advantages of having schools, as opposed to social settings where teachers direct learning without attendant pedagogical rights and student obligations. The circumstances which create the advantages of having schools do not always prevail, and sometimes nothing of value will be gained and perhaps something of value lost through the introduction of authority. So far as I can see, there are no grounds for creating the relevant rights and obligations where teachers and students do not differ substantially in their understanding of what is to be taught and everyone is like-minded about how to proceed. Finally, just because schooling implies a social setting in which teachers have the authority to teach, and there is ample reason to give them this authority, it does not follow that schools must or should have authority structures which leave out everyone except teachers. As Dearden points out, the authority to teach is one thing and the authority to settle disciplinary matters is another. In fact, the authority to teach can exist under regimes which most people would regard as involving students to an absurd degree. The problem of what authority structure befits the school is a difficult one which is not resolved merely be establishing the desirability of pedagogical authority. Unfortunately, that is a point which is not always appreciated, as we shall see in the final chapter.

I have tried to undermine the case for deschooling by exposing conceptual confusions which are liable to make it alluring and by pointing out educational advantages which are forfeited in doing away with schools. What remains to be considered is the proposal that we disestablish school, and nothing I have said so far discredits that proposal. However, I think that the deschoolers' arguments do not fare any better when they take this weaker position.

Illich's writings strongly emphasize the individualistic character of authentic educational achievement. Presumably, this is the general drift of passages such as the following: "But personal growth is not a measurable entity. It is growth in disciplined dissidence, which cannot be measured against any rod, or any curriculum, nor compared to someone else's achievement. In such learning one can emulate others only in imaginative endeavour, and follow in their footsteps rather than mimic their gait. The learning I prize is immeasurable re-creation."[10] This sort of language is likely to strike a responsive chord in contemporary hearts. The ideal of individuality is not only prized by the deschoolers; it is a shibboleth of our postromantic culture. And for those who adhere to that ideal, Illich's critique of compulsory schooling may be somewhat persuasive at this point. To the extent that all children are compelled to attend the same institution, each *must* submit to more or less the same experiences, the same rules, the same criteria of success and failure. The enforced uniformity of compulsory schooling might seem to be at odds with the idiosyncratic nature of "personal growth". An institution which all must attend is naturally designed with an eye to needs which are held in common, but if one's educational needs are apt to be unique and unpredictable, attendance will hardly be conducive to meeting them. If schooling were voluntary, at least I could get out when I perceived it was failing to meet my particular needs, but compulsion makes harm almost inevitable. In order to respect the individualistic nature of authentic educational achievement, the deschoolers advocate the creation of a range of social settings for education (including schools perhaps) to be used strictly according to individual preference.

This argument clearly will not do. First of all, the enforced uniformity of compulsory schooling need extend no further than the common experience of having to attend an institution which counts as a school. Students may or may not be subjected to precisely the same curriculum, the same discipline, procedures of assessment, and the like. Whatever can be said for or against identical treatment in these areas is entirely irrelevant to whether or not the principle of compulsory schooling is defensible. The real issue, then, is whether or not the rather modest requirement of compulsory schooling with respect to similar treatment for all students poses any substantial threat to individuality.

It is important to be very clear about what is meant by "individuality" in this context. Since we are dealing with an ideal which is to give shape to educational institutions, the interpretation we choose must capture something of substantial value. The only appealing interpretation I can envisage would locate individuality in the diverse array of forms of life which will almost certainly be exhibited in societies congenial to autonomy. Where individuals possess extensive liberty in choosing forms of life and are equipped to do so in a highly realistic and independent-minded fashion, conformity to the pattern of others' choices will not greatly influence the decisions they make. If it is also true that these individuals differ substantially in the lives to which they are naturally attracted and often find fulfilment by straying from the beaten path, a good deal of Illich's "disciplined dissidence" and "imaginative endeavour" is to be expected. But no argument I can find in the deschoolers' writings could lead us to believe that individuality, in the sense that connects it with autonomy, is endangered by the principle of compulsory schooling. To be sure, if one construes individuality as mere eccentricity, regardless of other considerations, then *any* instance of treating persons alike will appear to imperil individuality. But why on earth should we prize eccentricity per se? The answer to that question becomes glaringly obvious once it is realized that eccentricity may be shown in flouting just about *any* standard of value one might care to mention (including autonomy).

The deschoolers frequently deploy another argument for ending compulsion. Illich claims that schools (and he must mean compulsory schooling in this context) belong to a family of modern institutions which coerce their clients and deprive them of their status as free agents. In this respect, schooling is supposed to resemble imprisonment or enforced custody within psychiatric hospitals and the like.[11] Now whatever might be said in favour of prisons, they are not places where autonomy can be expected to prosper, in large part because coercion is virtually omnipresent. If compulsory schooling resembles prison as closely as Illich assumes, we can hardly suppose that autonomy will do any better there than it does in prison.

The disturbing force of this argument depends on the false assumption that compulsory schooling would have to be relentlessly coercive. Compulsion and coercion are very difficult concepts and although a thorough exploration of their complexities is out of place here, one salient difference bears upon our present concerns. If we wanted to determine whether a particular course of action was coerced, we would have to know something about the motives of the agent. Suppose someone eschews pornography in a society where it is available but forbidden by law. That is not enough to justify our saying that the law coerced the agent; it is not enough because these facts do not by themselves reveal why the individual shunned pornography in this instance. It could well be that the agent's religious convictions or sexual preferences determined her decision, and in that event there would have been no coercion. On the other hand, if she eschewed pornography because of the threat of legal sanctions, it would follow that coercion did occur. In civil society almost everyone will ordinarily act in conformity to the law, but it would be ridiculous to suppose that the extent of conformity coincides with an equally extensive coercion because the threat of legal sanctions is only necessary to explain conformity in a relatively small number of cases. The relevance of motivation to instances of coercion is brought out by the fact that "I was coerced" so often serves as an excuse which extenuates responsibility for one's actions. If one were coerced to steal, for example, it would follow that in the absence of a threat or coercive offer one would not have stolen; and in that case, personal responsibility for the theft shifts, at least partly, from the victim to the perpetrator of coercion.

However, threats can be made in situations where they are not motivationally necessary; and in such situations we can still legitimately speak of compulsion, even though the word "coercion" is out of place. All citizens in civil society are compelled to obey the law, even though not all are coerced to do so. In all western societies, children and adolescents within a certain age range are compelled to attend school, but not all are coerced to do so because many would attend even if they were not compelled. If I am coerced to do something I do it *despite* my desires; if I am compelled to do it I act *regardless* of my desires. Coerced actions are only a subset of compelled actions since the latter also subsumes compelled but un-coerced conduct.

It is not difficult to see why participation in an institution where coercion abounds is very likely to be destructive of autonomy. In circumstances of that kind one's conduct is persistently at variance with what would be chosen if threats or coercive offers did not exist. One's life comes to express the will of those who exercise coercion, and there will naturally be a tendency to lose confidence in the self as an independent centre of evaluation and choice. To be sure, some individuals survive the ordeal of the prison camp with their autonomy intact, but we admire such people precisely because the preservation of autonomy in the face of relentless coercion is immensely difficult. If compulsory schooling had to be as relent-lessly coercive as prisons, then Illich's demand that we disestablish school would be reasonable. But the deschoolers provide no grounds for believing that is so. In fact, conceivable and *prima facie* feasible varieties of compulsory schooling exist in which coercion is simply not ubiquitous. Coercion could not be prominent wherever teaching is devoted to developing students' interests and achieves at least moderate success. I pointed out earlier that as interest develops in an activity one necessarily acquires an increasingly strong motive for engaging in the activity, and threats or coercive offers will tend to become redundant. The idea that compulsory schooling should be devoted to developing students' interests is not incoherent, and I am not aware of any reason for supposing that it is unfeasible. Illich's association of compulsory schooling with various kinds of enforced custody may justify the rejection of certain kinds of com-pulsory schooling – viz., those permeated with coercion – but it cannot justify abandonment of the practice per se.

By debunking the arguments of the deschoolers one does not allay all the qualms likely to arise about compulsory schooling. There is a more academically respectable source of misgivings, and because these particular misgivings bear directly on the kind of defence of compulsion I shall mount, they deserve our attention.

In contemporary ethics, the two most widely discussed grounds for compulsion are the prevention of harm to persons other than the individual compelled and the promotion of the individual's own good. The need to avert harm to others will not carry us far in any defence of compulsory schooling. It would be silly to deny that failure to learn certain things in any culture will create a serious risk of such harm, and in contemporary western societies some of these things, though certainly not all, will require schooling. However, there is very little in the way of schooling which everyone or anyone in particular really must have in order to live in a manner which does not endanger the vital interests of other persons. True, there is a vast corpus of complex knowledge and skill – concerning agriculture and medicine, for example – which has to be transmitted to a large segment of each successive generation if catastrophe is to be avoided. But even though incentives for learners might sometimes be necessary to ensure transmission, compulsion is hardly called for. If an adequate moral education for all required a rich store of academic knowledge, then extensive compulsory schooling could be justified in order to safeguard the good of all; but I showed in the final section of chapter three that this is not required. Finally, it can be objected that a form of schooling, compulsory or otherwise, which treats the child merely as a potential risk to the well-being of others involves a culpable failure to acknowledge the institution's utility in furthering the child's *own* normative interest. For these reasons, any satisfactory argument for compulsory schooling is likely to rely heavily on the use of compulsion to further the good of those who are compelled.

This is where we get into trouble. Compulsion for the sake of the individual's own interests is widely discussed by contemporary moral philosophers not because it is thought to imply a very powerful reason for applying constraint. On the contrary, this variety of compulsion is believed to be especially pernicious, and philosophers have set themselves to circumscribe the supposedly narrow range of cases in which the practice just might be countenanced. The *locus classicus* for this approach is Mill's *On Liberty*.

The object of this essay is to assert one very simple principle as entitled to govern absolutely the dealings of society with the individual in the way of compulsion and control, whether the means used be physical force in the form of legal penalties, or the moral coercion of public opinion. That principle is, that the sole end for which mankind are warranted, individually or collectively, in interfering with the liberty of action of any of their number, is self-protection. That the only purpose for which power can be rightfully exercised over any member of a civilized community, against his will, is to prevent harm to others. His own good, either physical or moral, is not a sufficient warrant.[12]

The position Mill takes in the final sentence of this passage is slightly weaker than the one endorsed in the two sentences which immediately precede it. The earlier sentences imply that furthering the individual's own good could never be relevant at all to justify compulsion, whereas the final sentence entails only that it could never be enough to provide a justification. The weaker version would appear to be Mill's considered view because he does cite exceptions to his "one very simple principle." The weaker position is also the one widely adopted nowadays. An absolute prohibition on all acts which compel others to benefit them or avert self-inflicted harm is something that even ardent liberals cannot quite stomach, though there is a common conviction that something quite close to an absolute prohibition of such acts is desirable.

In contemporary philosophical parlance, the species of compulsion Mill decried is dubbed "paternalism." (I shall have something to say about this label later on, but for convenience I shall follow established philosophical usage.) Paternalism is not usually opposed now on the consequentialist grounds apparently favoured by Mill.[13] The argument against paternalism now tends to be largely in noncontingent terms. It is though that paternalistic acts are intrinsically evil in a way or to a degree that other acts curtailing liberty are not; that the distinctive evil of such acts resides in their violation of the agent's autonomy; and that the justification for paternalism depends not only on the desirability of its consequences but also, and crucially, on whether constraint is applied under conditions in which the intrinsic evil of the practice has been largely muted. Because it is assumed that a quasi-absolute embargo on paternalism is appropriate, the various attempts to specify the conditions under which it is justified have been marked by a concern to ensure that they will not often arise.[14]

These attempts have met with very doubtful success. One of the most well-known articles on the subject will illustrate the difficulties they have encountered. Joel Feinberg has offered the following basis for identifying cases of justified legal paternalism: "the state has the moral right to prevent wholly self-regarding conduct when, but only when, it is substantially nonvoluntary, or when temporary intervention is necessary to establish whether it is voluntary or not."[15] Feinberg does little to explain this murky distinction between substantially nonvoluntary and other kinds of behaviour, though it is certainly possible that the distinction could be made to fit a quasi-absolute embargo on paternalism. Perhaps Feinberg could specify tolerably clear and very easily satisfied criteria for conduct not substantially nonvoluntary (I shall refer to this as minimal voluntariness), and then argue that only on the infrequent occasions when conduct fails to meet the standard could paternalistic intervention be justified. The difficulty this creates is that if paternalistic intervention were unjustified whenever conduct is even minimally voluntary, it would become exceedingly difficult if not altogether impossible to justify compulsory schooling of more than negligible scope on paternalistic grounds.

Let me explain. Whatever content Feinberg might give to the concept of minimal voluntariness, he could not conceive of it in such a way that just because an adult or a child turns her back on some substantial benefit or inflicts some severe harm upon herself a lapse from the minimal standard occurs. In order to maintain a quasi-absolute embargo on paternalism, the pivotal concept in the theory would have to be explicated in such a way that the relevant minimal standard can and often is met by agents who act in a way at variance with their own good. Therefore, if it were shown that compulsory schooling for a certain number of years for a particular child brings benefits or prevents some self-inflicted harm that could not be a sufficient warrant for compulsion. In addition, one would need to show that compulsion forestalls choices not even minimally voluntary in a sense that is compatible with being very imprudent.

This imposes serious limitations on any paternalistic argument for compulsory schooling. It may be easy to show that the child who stays at home all day to watch television is being imprudent; it will be much harder to establish that her conduct is not minimally voluntary in the necessary sense. In short, even if Feinberg's theory could be developed to support Mill's qualified repugnance to pater-nalism, it would drastically curtail the scope of paternalistic poli-cies for the sake of educational ends.

Feinberg could object that the standards we use to differentiate justified and unjustified paternalism in the case of adults are not suitable for making that distinction in the case of children. In an-other article he appears to take a fairly indulgent approach to paternalism in our dealings with children.[16] Mill also makes it clear that his argument does not apply to children or other persons not in "the maturity of their faculties,"[17] and in this respect at least he would seem to have the support of common sense. Whatever doubts we might have about the morality of compelling adults for their own good, we commonly assume with Mill that a virtually unfettered paternalism is acceptable or even required in our rela-tions with children.

But there is good reason to believe that invoking a different stan-dard of justified paternalism for someone just because she is a child is morally indefensible discrimination. Customary or legal criteria determine the boundaries between childhood and adulthood – in our culture a certain age is reached, in others a rite of passage is

completed. John Kleinig has suggested that there are also normative concepts of childhood.[18] In other words, the distinction between
children and others sometimes allegedly hinges upon the presence
or absence of features supposed to have moral import, such as
maturity, rationality, and the like. It is true that we sometimes
describe immature or irrational adults as "children." But this is a
mere derogatory metaphor, parallel to sexists' condemnation of
weak-willed males as "women." What inspires such metaphors is
our beliefs (sometimes dangerously false beliefs) about what is typical or suitable in the conduct and character of women and children. Although these beliefs generate criteria of femininity and
childishness, they are not the same as concepts of womanhood or
childhood. It is wise to keep a firm grip on the distinction between
childishness and childhood because when it is lost sight of, the
Millian double standard on paternalism acquires a plausibility it
does not deserve.

Suppose we assume with Mill that uninhibited paternalism is
acceptable when human beings do not meet the normative condition of being in "the maturity of their faculties." This generates
much the same problem as Feinberg's notion of minimal voluntariness. If the assumption is to be reconciled with a quasi-absolute
prohibition of paternalism towards adults, then a *very* lax standard of maturity has to be adopted. If it is further assumed that
children will typically fail to meet the minimum standard of maturity, then failure to do so is also a defensible criterion of childishness. But it does not follow that uninhibited paternalism is
acceptable in dealing with this or that particular child because this
or that particular child may not be particularly childish. Although
children are, *ex hypothesi*, typically not yet minimally mature, it
cannot be doubted that many will be mature to the requisite degree. In the penumbral area of adolescence, minimal maturity
could well turn out to be far more common than childishness. It
will not help to claim that childhood as well as childishness are
morally relevant exceptions to the case against paternalism. This is
a futile manoeuvre because it runs into the insuperable difficulty of
showing how the mere fact of being a certain age makes a policy
acceptable that would otherwise be morally outrageous.

A more sophisticated move might be made at this point, though
it does nothing to redeem Mill's double standard. It can be argued
that though age, strictly speaking, is irrelevant to the distribution
of whatever moral right there might be to live without paternalistic compulsion, any attempt to determine who has the alleged right
directly on the basis of morally relevant considerations, such as

maturity, is fraught with grave moral risks. One can imagine maturity tests, for example, systematically biased against certain classes of persons or demeaning for all for who are subject to them or vulnerable to manipulation by testers.[19] If these evils were sufficiently weighty and intractable, the fiction of supposing that the right to be exempt from paternalism is only acquired at a certain age could be morally preferable to any method of identifying rightholders according to normative criteria. I shall examine a closely similar argument in the final section of the present chapter, and the point I shall make against it there parallels the one I shall make here. Even if the argument were cogent, it would still matter a great deal *which* age we selected. The age at which the right is "acquired" has to be chosen to minimize injustice towards children who are as normatively qualified as adults. Since the relevant normative qualification has to be very modest, whether it be minimal maturity, rationality, or voluntariness, the age we select will have to be decidedly low. Therefore, even from this perspective, the prospects of launching a paternalistic defence of compulsory schooling beyond the most limited objectives look extremely poor.

I do not believe there is any escape from this impasses so long as we accept Mill's quasi-absolute embargo on paternalism and the rationale for supporting the embargo which various contemporary philosophers have been trying to refine. There is an escape from this impasse, however, because there is good reason to reject the embargo and its rationale. The assumption that paternalistic acts are intrinsically evil in a way or to a degree that other acts restricting liberty are not is groundless, at least if the evil is thought to reside in some violation of the agent's autonomy. Once that assumption is dispensed with, it becomes clear that the distinction between justified and unjustified paternalism is going to depend on the balance of desirable and undesirable consequences. The alternative view I want to develop can yield a paternalistic argument for compulsory schooling of substantial scope, though it cannot authorize the cavalier attitude which philosophers and others have traditionally taken towards the freedom of children. But before I can present my case for compulsory schooling convincingly, I must defend the view of paternalism upon which it rests.

The assumption that paternalism offends autonomy more grievously than other acts of compulsion is open to different interpretations given that autonomy can be conceived in different ways. Feinberg argues that legal paternalism is evil because it "shows insufficient respect for [the individual's] autonomy, his right to govern himself at his own risk within his own moral domain."[20] In this sense "autonomy" designates a moral right which is possessed irrespective of one's character, rather than any particular ideal of character. But Feinberg affirms this right without showing why foregoing benefits or inflicting harm upon the self fall within one's own "moral domain," thereby begging rather than answering the question of whether or not paternalism is intrinsically evil. The endorsement of autonomy in Feinberg's sense is just another way of expressing an antipathy to paternalism since it provides no independent grounds for that antipathy. Paternalism could also be objected to because it interferes with the minimal autonomy which all subjects of choice instantiate. This could be Gerald Dworkin's position. He has recently maintained that paternalism entails "a usurpation of decision-making, either by preventing people from doing what they have decided or by interfering with the way in which they reach their decisions."[21] If this is thought to be intrinsically evil, it would explain Dworkin's desire to defend a position at least close to Mill's which he shows in his earlier essay on paternalism.[22] But paternalism is not unique among acts of compulsion in its usurpation of decision-making. Precisely the same usurpation occurs when compulsion is exercised for the sake of the interests of others. There is nothing in this notion of autonomy that could warrant singling out paternalism for denunciation.

If autonomy is construed as the personal ideal we have been concerned with throughout this book, does the case against paternalism look any better? I do not think that it does. It is important to bear in mind that what distinguishes paternalistic acts from others is what motivates an act of compulsion and justifies it in the eyes of the individual who exercises compulsion – the desire to benefit the individual compelled or avert self-inflicted harm. The actual consequences of the act are irrelevant to whether or not it counts as paternalistic. But whether or not an act of compulsion is significantly at odds with autonomy as a personal ideal is surely going to depend on its effects. The fact that compulsion is motivated and justified in someone's eyes by this rather than that makes no necessary difference to its constraining effects upon the development or exercise of autonomy.

Imagine that I am held under house arrest. This could be done in order to prevent harm to others. The authorities might believe that house arrest is the only feasible way of stopping me from provoking riots in a volatile political situation. It might also be done to protect me from harm. House arrest could be seen as a way of preventing me from confronting my political opponents in a manner certain to lead to my being lynched. In either event, the act of compulsion could have deleterious effects on the degree to which I am or will become autonomous, and it will certainly have an impact on the extent of my freedom. But in estimating the damage from the viewpoint of self-rule, the motives of those who put me under house arrest and what they believe justifies the action may not be relevant at all. By acting from this motive rather than another, the authorities' actions *could* have negative effects upon my self-rule which they would not otherwise have had. But this is merely a rather doubtful possibility. Paternalism cannot be objected to *a priori*, given that autonomy (as an ideal) is supposed to be the value we want to protect.[23]

It is still conceivable that a very powerful consequentialist objection to paternalism might be forthcoming which would apply to the vast majority of cases. This would vindicate Mill's position on his own terms without the noncontingent considerations which anti-paternalists have recently stressed. The nerve of Mill's attack on paternalism is his claim that people who have come into the maturity of their faculties are very likely to be better judges of their own normative interests than others.[24] In paternalism, the judgment of someone else as to what is in my interests has priority over mine, and because her judgment is very likely to be worse than mine, the act of compulsion is almost certain to do more harm than good. Mill's argument has been criticized on the grounds that it rests upon a naively optimistic view of the ability of individuals to discern what is in their interests.[25] This may well be true, but there is another basis to the argument which this criticism does not touch. Mill adopted a very tough-minded pessimism about our ability to make judgments about the good of others. People are the best judges of their own interests not because (or not *only* because) they are especially good at it, but because the competition is so awful. This strain of pessimism emerges strongly in passages such as the following: "In its interference with personal conduct [the public] is seldom thinking of anything but the enormity of acting or feeling differently from itself; and this standard of judgment, thinly disguised, is held up to mankind as the dictate of religion and philosophy by nine-tenths of all moralists and speculative writers."[26] In practice, paternalism is just a license for tyranny in that it provides a facade of righteousness for attempts to enforce a deadening social uniformity. There are large empirical assumptions here, but if they held any truth, it would appear that Mill's argument is one that cannot be viewed lightly once we take the ideal of autonomy seriously. I have already argued that the values of autonomy and individuality connect in important ways. If paternalism in practice were just a way of destroying individuality, it would be certain to cause havoc to the cultivation of autonomy.

Now even if Mill's empirical assumptions were well founded, he would not have a cogent argument against paternalistic as opposed to other kinds of compulsion. If I conceived the good of others to be incompatible with their acting or feeling differently from me, my paternalistic interventions in their lives would doubtless be highly tyrannical. But so too would my attempts to stop anyone from harming others because what I consider harmful would be distorted by my egregious intolerance. Suppose I prevented someone from practising a religion different from mine on the grounds that practising it was self-inflicted harm. The same conception of the good of others which would underpin my paternalism could also be employed to argue that compulsion in this case prevented harm to others by protecting innocent people from the baneful example of someone engaging in a diabolical perversion of worship.

Mill's argument does illustrate the way in which acts of compulsion which presuppose judgments about the good of others are apt to be disastrous if the judgments are seriously flawed. Perhaps because the general public in Victorian England did not prize autonomy and individuality in the lives of others, this led to many deprivations of freedom with profoundly undesirable consequences. Maybe similar things could be said about some contemporary societies. But if a lesson is to be learnt from these supposed facts it is not that we should have a quasi-absolute embargo on all acts of compulsion which presuppose judgments about the good of others. Rather, we have to ensure that compulsion is informed by a defensible conception of the good of others. In particular, we will have to show due regard for the importance of others living in such a way that autonomy can prosper. This suggests a parallel between some of Illich's strictures upon schooling and Mill's rejection of paternalism. Illich abjures schooling, but most of his criticisms only apply to particular species of that genus. He seems incapable of imagining a form of schooling which would not have those undesirable features he rightly deplores – autocratic teaching, inflexible curricula, and so on. Mill's critique of paternalism shows a similar failure of imagination. His argument applies only to a particular variety of paternalism, but it is used to support the grandiose claim that all or at least virtually all paternalism should be abandoned.

Mill's tendency to blur the distinction between paternalism per se and forms of the practice corrupted by a defective conception of the good of others has lingered in contemporary discussions of the topic. This is apparent, for example, in the very fact that "paternalism" is now the accepted term for the form of compulsion Mill deprecated.[27] So far as I am aware, it has never been noted that this involves a significant departure from nonphilosophical usage of the word. In ordinary language "paternalism" does not connote a certain type of compulsion or any other class of actions; it designates a particular, morally offensive attitude.[28] If I were describing a senior colleague, say, it matters a great deal whether I choose to describe him as paternalistic or fatherly. "Paternalistic" has pejorative overtones which "fatherly" lacks. Why? The fatherly colleague, one imagines, is ready to share his knowledge and experiences with neophytes to the profession, sympathetic and helpful when they blunder, and pleased by their successes. In other words, his attitude to just what one would expect of a decent father when a grown-up child has launched upon a career. "Paternalistic", however, conjures up a very different and far less honourable image. The paternalistic senior colleague treats his juniors not as if they were his own grown-up children, but as if they were still childish. One imagines someone high-handed and meddlesome, who assumes that younger colleagues have no capacity to shoulder responsibilities on their own, and no right to be consulted when decisions which bear upon their interests are being made. In short, the paternalist, in the ordinary pejorative sense of that word, is someone who takes the view that another person is largely incapable of looking after her own interests or of showing due concern for the interests of others. Paternalism also requires that this view of the other's good be mistaken and that the view pervades the paternalists' behaviour towards the other. It is obvious that people who take this attitude will frequently act paternalistically, in the philosophical sense; and since their view of the other's good does not sufficiently acknowledge the other's autonomy, one can safely expect the dire consequences Mill predicted where such action is taken. Now the connection between the two senses of "paternalism" is by no means water-tight. The mere fact that I compel someone to do something for her own good is no reason to believe that my attitude towards here is paternalistic. After all, paternalistic attitudes can also be expected to give rise to extensive unjustified compulsion which purports to prevent harm to others. But just because I deprive someone of liberty in order to shield someone else from harm does not mean I have any morally offensive attitude towards the person I compel.

It would not matter at all that the philosophical concept of paternalism differs from what we find in ordinary language if the two concepts were carefully distinguished. But they are not. Consider the following passage from the very beginning of Feinberg's seminal essay:

The principle of legal paternalism justifies state coercion to protect individuals from self inflicted harm, or in its extreme version, to guide them, whether they like it or not, toward their own good ... Legal paternalism seems to imply that since the state often can know the interests of citizens better than they know themselves, it stands as a permanent guardian of those interests *in loco parentis*. Put in this way, paternalism seems a preposterous doctrine. If adults are treated like children they will come in time to be like children.[29]

If we endorse the principle affirmed in Feinberg's first sentence, we are not carried inexorably to the sorry state of affairs described in his final sentence. Feinberg says that the principle "seems to imply" that the state often has better knowledge of what is good for citizens than the citizens themselves. But the principle makes no reference at all to the frequency with which the agents of the state might have such knowledge. So why does Feinberg find that implication? The answer would appear to lie in the last sentence of the passage. Here Feinberg is talking about treating those who are not really "like children" as if they were, and the corrosive effects that is likely to have on their self-image. In other words, he is talking about paternalism in its nonphilosophical sense, and it is certainly true that those who evince that attitude will believe that they often understand the interests of others better than the others themselves. But this does nothing to discredit the principle specified in the opening sentence because Feinberg has simply changed the subject. Whatever persuasiveness the passage might have is specious insofar as it depends upon an equivocation between two senses of the word "paternalism". I suspect that the same equivocation is behind Feinberg's assumption, which so many other writers have advanced, that paternalism involves a grave intrinsic evil because it violates autonomy in some morally central sense. In that it involves a culpable derogation of another's capacity to flourish as a person, the attitude of paternalism signifies contempt for the other's very personhood – and whatever consequences might flow from displaying the attitude in particular circumstances, it would still count as a serious intrinsic evil. But this tells us nothing about the intrinsic disvalue of compelling someone for her own good.

If we take the view that paternalism (in the philosophical sense) is justified whenever the desirable consequences outweigh the undesirable ones, we do not open the door to the creation of some

Brave New World through massive social engineering. The telling objection to such a world does not hinge on any general objection to paternalism; it rather derives from certain views about what are desirable and undesirable consequences. Huxley's Brave New World is built on the assumption that the only thing of value in human life is a sort of bovine contentment, and on any even faintly plausible conception of value, that is an appalling mistake. In fact, if we approach the problem of compulsion in light of the theory of the value of freedom outlined in this book, there are ample grounds for believing that it will not lead to a paternalism of an intuitively excessive scope.

My theory would suggest that paternalistic compulsion is justified if it renders the compelled individual more autonomous or maximizes her liberty, and these benefits are not outweighed by the policy's undesirable consequences. These conditions carry certain obvious implications for the way policy-makers should proceed in this area. First of all, the exercise of compulsion has to be tempered by an awareness that the benefits we hope to bring about or the self-inflicted harm we hope to prevent can hardly be guaranteed in advance. For example, if we were considering the possibility of forcing responsibility for an important decision upon someone who had deeply entrenched habits of deference and intense fears about making independent choices, then the likelihood of our action effecting a higher degree of autonomy, instead of just traumatizing and humiliating the individual, may be very slight. Indeed, whenever possible paternalistic interventions go against the grain of long-settled inclinations and tendencies – and they will very frequently do so in the case of adults – it is unlikely that our good intentions will be fulfilled. There is another reason why we should be sceptical about our ability to exercise compulsion for the sake of the individual compelled. In chapter two, I connected the concept of personal autonomy with the individual's attempt to bestow meaning upon her life, and stressed the role of her interests in this regard. I also tried to show that the extent of her overall freedom is contingent on the extent to which she can freely express her current interests or initiate certain kinds of self-transformation. It follows that whether or not a particular act of compulsion helps to bring about a higher level of autonomy or maximizes freedom will depend in part upon facts about the mental states of the person who is compelled. These facts are far less than transparent to others and they can be expected to vary substantially across different lives. Admittedly, we now know enough about self-deception and the like to realize that we are often mistaken about our own mental states.

But it is still reasonable to assume that the facts concerning the individual's mental state are generally rather less opaque to the individual herself than they are to others. Furthermore, paternalistic legislation can only show little sensitivity to variation in the law's effects across different lives without becoming hopelessly unwieldy. This creates a serious risk that the legislation will cause a good deal of unintended harm. The fact that autonomy can be cultivated in radically different lives, some of which will inevitably strike any one of us as utterly alien or even repellant, also gives us reason to be cautious about adopting paternalistic policies. Such policies do give dangerous scope to our desire to make others like ourselves, even though there is no logical connection between that desire and paternalism as Mill thought. In dealings with our own children, for example, the temptation to mould the loved one in one's own image is especially pressing, and it doubtless causes much tyranny under the aegis of paternalism. A constant vigilance against this temptation would serve as a significant brake upon the extension of paternalistic practices in morally unacceptable directions.

When paternalistic interference is being contemplated, uncertainty about our ability to do any good is apt to be combined with awareness that some harm will flow from interference. Although this will be difficult to predict in advance, given that the prospective object of intervention is a subject of choice, certainly our action will constrain someone in exercising a degree of personal autonomy. If the intervention also prevents the individual from freely expressing some deeply held interest, it exacts a nontrivial loss of freedom. The benefits of interference could more than countervail the evil in this loss, but where the benefits cannot be foreseen with any justifiable confidence, paternalism is sheer recklessness.

These caveats cannot support anything close to an absolute prohibition of paternalistic compulsion. It is not hard to imagine circumstances in which some or all of them would carry little force. In particular, due regard for these caveats is compatible with an argument for compulsory schooling of substantial scope. And we are now in a position to look at that argument.

Chapter three stressed the value of schooling in enlarging the scope of students' freedom. I shall adhere to the same emphasis in my defence of compulsory schooling. More precisely, I shall argue that the main reason for compulsory schooling is its capacity to maximize the freedom of students.

The possibility that paternalistic interference could be justified by maximizing the freedom of the compelled individual has not been viewed sympathetically by many philosophers.[30] This probably has to do with the common acceptance of the traditional criterion of constraint in policy discussion. It is only in fairly unusual circumstances that a particular act of interference with someone's choices will have the effect of forestalling even greater external interference with the individual's choices. Perhaps that is true of laws against slavery in most cases, but it will hardly be true of compulsory schooling. The amount of external interference which I encounter in life – coercion, physical confinement, and so forth – is unlikely to be minimized by what I am compelled to learn at school. On the other hand, if the correct conception of relevant constraint implies that the abilities fostered through compulsory schooling do increase our freedom, then the possibility of that policy securing more freedom than it takes away becomes readily apparent. But an argument for compulsory schooling will have to establish its superiority over purely voluntary systems. It is conceivable that voluntary schooling would be liberating, and that benefits would be achieved without the costs to freedom which compulsion imposes. So why favour compulsion?

Suppose we have a schooling system which is at least moderately successful in developing students' interests. Nevertheless, if an individual has no desire to develop her interests, then she may not want to attend. Even when the desire is present, it might not prevail against competing inclinations unless it is supported through compulsion. Indulging passing whims and likings may be far more agreeable than the disciplined and often arduous business of developing one's interests. By allowing someone to do whatever she wills, there is no reason to suppose that the latter would be chosen. Indeed, it is simply irrational to expect anyone to grasp securely the point of developing an interest in the absence of substantial knowledge and experience. If what I value is simple and easily achieved, the attraction of what is more complex and only attained with difficulty will not be irresistible. Therefore, the less developed someone's interests are, the more likely it is that she will not desire or have an insufficiently strong desire to make extensive use of voluntary schooling. It follows from this that the educational benefits of attending school are least likely to accrue to those who are most in need of them. In early childhood, just about everyone will be in this state of acute need because their interests will virtually all be at a primitive stage of development. The only reliable way of ensuring the liberating effects of schooling will be through compulsion. Otherwise, any child's education will be liable to degenerate into projects abandoned when they become too difficult and interests never pushed far enough to realize much of their value.

It is worth noting that none of this presupposes the controversially bleak view of the nature of children which radical educational theorists are apt to ascribe (sometimes rightly) to the advocates of compulsion. I do not assume that children are utterly impervious to reason and therefore have to be forced to do what is good for them. On the contrary, even if a child is eminently rational, my argument may still apply. If the values one is familiar with are not the sort of thing which depend upon perseverance, subtle discriminations, and so on, then it is perfectly sensible to forego activities which make such demands. Others may tell one that these activities become deeply engrossing once enough effort is put into them. But there are no grounds for supposing that such an argument should be accepted unless one *already* wants to develop one's interests, and the presence of that desire in any robust form cannot be taken for granted. For example, if I am beginning to find the music I habitually listen to rather stale and repetitive and I long for novel musical experiences, then I have good reason to take the advice of a friend who proclaims the virtues of some difficult composer I have never tried seriously. But if I am content with the current range of my musical appreciation, there is nothing even mildly unreasonable about my determination to stick with composers I have already tried. The same point applies, *mutatis mutandis*, to children who have yet to see the point of developing even very primitive interests any further.

It would appear that there are conditions in which compulsory as opposed to voluntary schooling is justified on the grounds that compulsion would maximize the freedom of those compelled. But just what is the scope of justified compulsion on these grounds? It would be foolish for anyone to give a precise answer which is supposed to be universally applicable. A defensible precise answer will depend upon empirical facts which will hardly be invariant from one context to another, and philosophers are no experts when it comes to such facts. Nevertheless, I believe it is possible to say something nontrivial about the issue of scope without begging any really contestable empirical question. In order to get some sense of the strengths and limitations of the kind of argument for compulsion I am exploring, it will be useful to contrast a situation in which the argument very obviously warrants compulsion with one in which it does not.

Miriam has no clear idea of what her interests are, much less any inkling of what might be gained from wisely directed attempts to develop any one of them. A number of years of compulsory schooling would change that. Miriam would be freed to do an ample range of things she would become deeply interested in doing, and here life would be characterized by a degree of self-rule that otherwise would not have even been approached. Moreover, the freedom compulsion takes away cannot count for much because the possibility of choice it forecloses could not instantiate more than negligible autonomy. Only a desire to wallow in her own anomie could explain a desire not to go to school. Insofar as it detracts from her range of open options, a law compelling attendance at school in these circumstances would not be very dissimilar from a law prohibiting the use of heroin. In short, what we have is a trade-off between the disvalue of a modest loss of freedom entailed by compulsion and a substantial gain which could not have been experienced without compulsion. Given that we should maximize freedom, the trade-off is plainly desirable, at least other things being equal.

Michelle has already attended school for several years. What she has learnt has deepened her interests in certain areas. But she has no desire to continue this process any further, at least for the present. Now this lack of desire does not signify any lapse from the ideal of autonomy. There is nothing in the concepts of realism or independence of mind which commits us to unrelenting effort in extending our interests in new directions. If we are reluctant to respect Michelle's decision, I suspect that it will stem from a commitment to a somewhat different ideal than autonomy. An attractive conception of the good enjoins human beings to push their talents and interests to the very utmost in order to live with the maximum vigour and intensity of which they are capable. This ideal of self-perfection is often conflated with autonomy – for example, the two are deeply entangled in Mill's famous third chapter of *On Liberty* – but they are distinct ideals for all that. Self-perfection can be autonomously embraced, but it can be autonomously repudiated as well. And there is no reason to suppose that lives governed by a restless drive to perfect the self are necessarily superior to those which place greater emphasis on the values of repose, familiarity, and stability.

So Michelle's freedom to leave school is not to be dismissed as something of little consequence in the estimation of her liberty. Moreover, the potential liberating effects of continuing to enforce attendance in this case are at best very uncertain. Michelle's desire to leave school is good evidence that much educational success is unlikely to be forthcoming if compulsion persists because her desire is shaped by substantial self-knowledge and an informed sense of what school has to offer. It would seem that the caveats about paternalistic compulsion outlined at the end of the immediately preceding section carry a good deal of force here. Further compulsory schooling for Michelle would result in a serious loss of freedom in the present for the sake of highly speculative gains in the future. The presumptive principle of liberty could not justify that policy.

There could be very many students whose situation is in other respects very similar to Michelle's but who do not desire to leave school. It is worth noting that in their case, because compulsion is simply unnecessary, the presumptive principle could not warrant the loss of freedom they would endure through compulsion. It will not do to object that this is a trivial loss. Compulsion prevents them from *freely* pursuing their own education, and insofar as that is something they are interested in doing as substantially autonomous agents, their loss of freedom is a significant one.

The cases I have briefly examined illustrate the relevance of three considerations in determining whether compulsory schooling can be supported on the grounds that it will maximize freedom. First, is the extent to which we can be reasonably sure that compulsory schooling will bring a substantial accession of freedom. Second, is the question whether compulsory, as opposed to voluntary schooling is needed in order to secure these benefits. Third, the loss to freedom which compulsion requires has to be estimated, and a crucial consideration here will be the extent to which compulsion forecloses possibilities of choice that might have been autonomously exploited by the individual compelled.

Given the importance of this last consideration, it is clear that there is a very familiar kind of situation in which protracted compulsion would seem warranted, even where its predictable benefits are slight or highly uncertain. It is extremely doubtful that compulsory schooling eliminates possibilities of choice which count for much by the standard of self-rule if, upon leaving school, one is likely to be both highly vulnerable to the effects of a popular culture often inimical to personal autonomy and permanently consigned to a lowly position in the socio-economic hierarchy where work is sheer drudgery. In these social conditions, prospective drop-outs who fit Michelle's description may be rather rare. If indeed these grim alternatives are the *only* feasible ones for a particular student, one certainly cannot rule out the possibility that further compulsion is desirable. Nevertheless, there are appalling dangers in this way of thinking because it lends itself to indefensi-

ble interference once it is uncritically assumed that the grim alternative to further compulsion is inescapable. Frequently, it is not.
There is no reason to suppose that conditions outside the school
which are destructive of autonomy are completely intractable. If
we prize self-rule for our children, it is far from obvious that the
fitting response to the prospective drop-out is further compulsion,
rather than providing richer opportunities for meaningful work
and leisure outside the school. The evil consequences of dropping
out can also be mitigated by policies which secure easier access to
school later in life or create incentives for further voluntary attendance. There is a tendency to think that the only reliable way of
safeguarding the good of our children is through compulsion. This
might make sense based on some conceptions of their good, but it
does not do so if we wish them to prosper as autonomous agents.

There is another reason for believing that paternalistic policies
derived from the ideal of autonomy will not always lead to compulsory schooling of the scope we now complacently accept. Consider
once again the case where compulsion was incontestably appropriate. If our only options were to send Miriam to school for ten years,
say, or else allow her to wallow in her own anomie, then the presumptive principle would warrant compulsion. But this is an artifi-
cially circumscribed set of options. Why not compel her to attend
for only nine years, or eight, or seven? The question is deeply relevant because we cannot expect that less than ten years will mean
utter educational failure for her. On the contrary, because whatever success we can expect will be gradually realized, after five or
six years of compulsion, say, there may well be little or no relevant
difference between Miriam's and Michelle's situations should the
latter decide she wants no more school. The more educational success, the less reason we have to suppose that compulsion can be
defended on the grounds that it maximizes freedom.

It will be objected that my argument in this section is vitiated by
the assumption that we could determine the scope of justifiable
compulsory schooling on a case by case basis by asking about the
likely effects of further compulsion on the individual's freedom.
But in practice this might turn out to be a hopelessly unwieldy and
destructive course. I alluded earlier to the fact that if a moral right
against paternalistic interference existed, any attempt to determine who has it directly on the basis of possibly relevant normative
criteria, such as maturity, could cause far more harm than good. A
parallel claim could be made about attempts to determine the
scope of compulsory schooling directly on the basis of its prospects
for maximizing freedom. The considerations I have identified

which count for or against an act of compulsion enlarging the range of someone's freedom are not so precise that we could easily develop standardized procedures for weighing them which would not, for example, illicitly discriminate against certain social groups or be subject to frequent abuse by those who employ the procedures. Therefore, the current practice of compelling children to attend school for ten years or so might well be thoroughly defensible, even if there are some or even many children who fit Michelle's description long before their ten years is up. The current practice might be defensible – at least if it were combined with a genuinely beneficial curriculum – because its associated evils are less than those we could expect to flow from attempts to regulate compulsion directly on the basis of its conduciveness to greater freedom.

It should be noted that this argument contains much sheer speculation. Of course, it is not speculative to maintain that assigning the obligation to attend school on the normative basis I have recommended is going to be associated with some unavoidable evils. Only the silliest optimist could deny that. It is another matter to suppose that the status quo involves fewer undesirable consequences than any feasible method of applying the normative considerations I favour. But I do not want to press that point here since the contradictory supposition is also highly speculative. What I do want to stress is that if age is the best feasible standard for deciding who should and should not be obliged to attend school, it will not be because it provides a genuinely independent alternative to the normative considerations I have been discussing. The age we select has to be determined by relevant normative considerations.

How could we set about justifying the claim that compulsory schooling, say between the ages of six and sixteen, is morally preferable to any other way of deciding who should be compelled to go to school? Clearly, we have to gather whatever evidence is available about the extent to which morally unjustified paternalistic interference is avoided through this policy and justified interventions are ensured. But the distinction between unjustified and justified acts in this context will hinge at least partly on whether or not the freedom of those compelled will be maximized. It will not do to reply that our quantitative judgments about freedom are too uncertain and imprecise to be deemed relevant here at all, however conceptually scrupulous we are in making them. Exactly the same point could be made against *any* other plausible normative basis for distinguishing between justified and unjustified paternalism – minimal voluntariness, maturity, rationality, and the like. And if we dismiss all such grounds for evaluating acts of paternalism, then we have no grounds for believing that ten years of schooling is morally preferable to fifty or half a day.

It is important to see that age does not provide an independent alternative to normative considerations in determining the scope of compulsory schooling because if we believe that it does, this will tend to insulate current practice from criticism derived from those considerations. We shall blithely accept the fate of the many children who fit Michelle's description but are still compelled to attend school. Any attempt to remedy their fate by determining the scope of compulsion on normative grounds would take us out of the frying pan and into the fire, or so we shall suppose. But far fewer children might endure the fate of Michelle if the age at which compulsion ends were pushed downwards. In other words, if age is indeed the best feasible basis for settling the scope of compulsory schooling, the specific provisions we make must still be designed to achieve an optimum balance between morally justified and unjustified acts of compulsion.

It is not hard to envisage just how this might work in practice. Suppose for the first three or four years of compulsory schooling, beginning roughly at the age it now begins, the presumptive principle of liberty would justify compulsion for most, perhaps even virtually all students. Within this age range, compulsion would be uncontroversially justified. If there is at least a moderate level of success within the schooling system and conditions outside are not thoroughly unpropitious, then after nine or ten years of attendance, say, it is reasonable to expect that students will be fairly autonomous, have some intensively developed interests, and so on. In that event, continued compulsion will be clearly unwarranted, both for those who wish to continue attending and for those who do not. But real difficulties are likely to arise within a substantial age range between these two extremes. Within this problematical area, judgments about how the presumptive principle applies to particular cases will very frequently be impossible to make with any assurance of being right. Therefore, it would appear that powerful generalizations about how the principle would apply to any specific age within the problematical range cannot be made.

How are we to proceed? In an article on the transition from childhood to adulthood, Francis Schrag has argued that the decisive factor in determining majority status should be "whether the age that is set is perceived to be reasonable by both majors and minors alike."[31] Schrag points out that extensive damage is likely to be done to "public confidence in public processes and procedures" where there is a marked discrepancy between perceptions of what age rightly marks the transition to majority status and the age which actually does so in law. In the same vein, one might argue that an important consideration in determining the scope of compulsory schooling should be the perceptions of all affected parties – parents, students, and teachers especially – about what age limits are reasonable. Indeed, it might be argued that this should be the only consideration, and not just one that comes into play alongside others, such as the presumptive principle of freedom. Where a serious disparity exists between the actual scope of compulsion and public perceptions of what is reasonable, this could be expected to breed alienation from the schooling system and thereby militate against its success. Schrag notes that perceptions will change from one context to another and it will be necessary to effect some kind of compromise between the view of different segments of the public. But it does seem fair to assume that if this consideration were brought to bear in determining the scope of compulsory schooling under present conditions, it would probably support something pretty close to the status quo.

My major objection to Schrag's argument and any attempt to recast it as a solution to the problem of the scope of compulsory schooling is this: if public perceptions about the reasonableness of social arrangements are relevant to their justification, the weight we attach to them must surely depend on what we know about the soundness of these perceptions. Not long ago all women were denied full majority status in western societies because none could acquire the legal right to vote. Before this injustice was rectified, there was no doubt a time when public perceptions would have supported the denial of suffrage to women. Schrag could argue that even someone who recognized the injustice of this situation would still have had to reckon with the harm that might be done to "public confidence in public processes and procedures" by efforts to force respect for women's moral rights upon a deeply reluctant public. This is certainly true, but it is simply wrong to assume *a priori* that the decisive consideration in any decision should be public perception of what is reasonable even where these perceptions are untenable. Likewise, it cannot be assumed that the scope of compulsory schooling should be dictated by public perceptions if these turn out to be faulty.

It might be conceded that this is enough to establish that the kind of argument Schrag develops is not the last word on when majority status should be granted or compulsory schooling ended. But it is still possible that public perceptions should be decisive when other normative considerations are not at variance with them. Perhaps that is all Schrag would claim for his argument since he presents it only after reaching the conclusion, prematurely in my view, that other plausible grounds for setting the age of majority turn out to be useless upon reflection. Therefore, one might claim that deference to public opinion is desirable within that substantial age range where it appears that powerful generalizations cannot be made about whether paternalistic intervention is warranted on the basis of the value of maximizing freedom.

But the presumptive principle of liberty can be of more use than this conclusion would suggest. I argued earlier that as compulsory schooling progresses, the case for compulsion as a means of maximizing the individual's freedom becomes gradually weaker, given increasing educational success. If there is a substantial age range within which we are uncertain as to how the principle would apply, we can still be quite sure that the case for compulsion will tend to be significantly weaker towards the end of the range than it is at the beginning. At least we can be sure that once schooling is bringing the educational success it is supposed to bring, and where it is not, the possibility of compulsory attendance being paternalistically defended is decidely remote. Insofar as we are concerned with regulating compulsion to maximize freedom, how are we to acknowledge the moral relevance of the fact that compulsion becomes increasingly less likely to be defensible as the higher end of the age range is approached? I suggest that an appropriate acknowledgment of this fact would be to gradually diminish the duration of compulsory schooling as the age increases. For example, older children might be compelled to attend for fewer hours a day or fewer days a week. The rationale for this policy would be the principle that where the case for compulsion is weaker, the compulsion should at least be less intrusive.

I suspect that this principle, or something very like it, is already widely accepted. Where the grounds for paternalistic interference are especially weighty – in the case of prohibitions on the use of very dangerous drugs, for example – we are apt to accept draconian rigour in the way compulsion is exerted. We are ready to countenance jail terms, mandatory rehabilitation programs, the seizure of property, and the like because so much is at stake. Where the grounds for paternalistic interference are rather weaker, measures of this kind strike us as intolerably intrusive. It may well be desirable to have legislation prescribing the use of seat belts in automobiles. But jail terms for those who break the law is surely going a bit too far. Because the intrusiveness of compulsory schooling will depend in large part on how much of one's time must be devoted to attending, it is reasonable to argue that as the grounds for compulsion weaken, the duration of obligatory attendance should be correspondingly reduced. In the case of children after six or so years of schooling, we might reasonably doubt that abandoning compulsion altogether would be the best course, given the value of enhancing their self-rule; but even if compulsion is to continue, the increasing weakness of the case for doing so gives us a strong reason to apply compulsion in a less intrusive fashion.

If this were done under present circumstances, the practice would probably run foul of public perceptions of what is reasonable. But it hardly follows that this is a good enough reason to abandon the practice. It is very far from obvious that the moral costs of maintaining an unjustifiably intrusive form of paternalism are worth paying in order to avoid whatever harm might follow from adopting a course against public perceptions in this instance. Furthermore, even if this trade-off were the best choice, we would still have good reason for attempting to change public perceptions to bring them into line with the limits of defensible paternalism.

CHAPTER FIVE

The Government of Schooling

It would be possible to implement the policies for schooling I defended in chapters three and four within the context of benevolent despotism. A curriculum which is interest-based in the sense I have recommended and compulsion which is kept within the limits of morally permissible paternalism could both be realized without extending any authority to students within schools. But sometimes the child-centred demand for the liberation of childhood has been heard within discussion about the government of schooling itself. Giving students a voice within the authority structure certainly brings new burdens and responsibilities into the lives of students, but it also ushers in new freedoms which have sometimes been thought important to their education. This is the final theme of the child-centred tradition I shall address.

I want to show that extensive student participation in the government of schooling, and perhaps even full-blown democratic schooling, become reasonable policies to adopt under conditions which should not be difficult to realize. The central point I shall make is that under these conditions there is good reason for according authority to students because they are likely to use it competently. Like the arguments of chapters three and four, this one ultimately depends upon the value of autonomy, even though for the first three sections of the chapter that concept will not figure in my reasoning. These sections lay necessary groundwork for the moves I shall make as the chapter draws to a close.

It may appear to be the height of folly to launch an argument of this kind in the absence of reliable empirical investigation of the effects of student participation under the relevant circumstances. As far as I am aware, there has been no such investigation. A large and very interesting body of empirical research on workplace de-

mocracy does exist,[1] but the dangers of drawing on this to support
the conclusion I wish to defend are too obvious to be worth spelling
out. As a result, some of the premises of my reasoning, and hence its
conclusion, are tinged with speculation. I do not apologize for this.
My empirical premises are, I believe, either platitudinous or at
least highly plausible. At any rate, I am in good company among
contemporary philosophers of education in my willingness to engage in a bit of empirical speculation, notwithstanding frequent
claims about the importance of confining our attention to conceptual matters. *In Ethics and Education*, R.S. Peters dismisses the
possibility of delegating authority to students or even consulting
them about the curriculum and the competence of staff in a couple
of sentences, on the grounds that their immaturity makes them
unfit for either authority or consultation.[2] The brusqueness with
which Peters dismisses this possibility tends to blur the fact that
his position rests upon empirical assumptions which are not irrefu-
table, to say the least. Are students at all levels of schooling so
egregiously immature that they are not even fit to be consulted
about their own curriculum? I think the answer to this is obvious,
though it is not the answer which Peters's argument requires. But
my purpose in raising this point is not primarily to criticize Peters;
it is rather to illustrate the fact that philosophers of education who
want to say something important about the government of schooling can hardly do so without departing, though perhaps not overtly,
from the ideal of "pure" philosophy which analytic practitioners
have usually espoused. What follows does not pretend to be "pure"
philosophy, but it may be convincing for all that.

At the outset I should explain what I mean by "democratic schooling." There is as little consensus within contemporary political
science and philosophy about how "democracy" is to be defined and
applied as there is within ordinary political discourse. However, I
trust that I shall identify one kind of regime for the school with
enough precision that what I have in mind will be tolerably clear,
even if the appellation "democratic" is inevitably open to dispute.

I assume that in a democratic institution authoritative decisions
are determined, or at least closely regulated, by procedures in
which the voice of each insider carries equal weight and other
voices are excluded. Where all decisions are made through such
procedures, pure participatory democracy exists. But the democracies we are likely to be acquainted with do not fit that description. In virtually every case, some fields of authority will be

confined to only some individuals, despite the fact that their decisions might be at odds with what would have been the outcome of deliberations in which each insider had an equal voice. Yet inequalities of authority must be regulated in a certain way by these egalitarian deliberations if democracy is to be preserved. The right of some individuals to have more authority than others must be periodically bestowed or revoked through deliberations of the relevant kind, or else it must be delegated, as in the case of civil servants hired by elected representatives, by those whose special authority does come from a collective decision by insiders.

I have said that democracy involves the inclusion of insiders within the authority structure and the exclusion of others. It is not hard to see that some distinction of this kind is essential to the concept. For example, we would surely be destroying the democratic character of the state if we withheld the right to vote from all persons who lack university degrees of sold it to wealthy foreigners who wanted to influence our political process. It is conceivable that these policies could be desirable; it is not conceivable that their implementation would be compatible with democracy. Lacking a university degree is patently not sufficient reason for being an outsider in the necessary sense, and a willingness to buy the right to vote is not sufficient to make one an insider. But in many other situations the distinction is very difficult to discern. In the case of migrant workers who have been quasi-permanent residents in a particular country, it is not clear whether their exclusion from the political process detracts from its democratic credentials. When applying the concept of workplace-democracy we make assumptions about whether the exclusion of apprentices, say, or part-time employees conforms to democratic rule, though I do not think we yet have a sufficiently precise and defensible account of the distinction between outsiders and insiders to support these assumptions adequately. Providing such account would be no easy matter, and I have no intention of attempting to do so here. But I shall make some assumptions about who counts as insiders and outsiders in the context of schooling, and my assumptions are somewhat controversial.

It has been thought that democratic rule for schools would include representatives of the local community, parents, as well as students and teachers.[3] Because the kind of regime I have in mind is confined to students and teachers, something should be said about why I have disregarded the local community and parents. The local community and society at large doubtless have a stake in what happens at school. If schools were run so ineptly that they produced a generation of ignorant delinquents, then we would all suffer dearly. But having a stake in the way authority is used or abused in a particular social setting is not enough to make one an insider in the relevant sense. Peters has suggested that the democratic state implies "some established procedure by means of which those who suffer from state action can be consulted and can bring their desires and opinions to bear upon it."[4] But if all who suffer from Saudi Arabia's control of oil production could bring their desires and opinions to bear within its political process, this would not make Saudi Arabia more democratic; it would rather signal the partial dissolution of the Saudi state within some international political structure. Likewise, if everyone who had a stake in what happens at school were given an equal voice in its government, this would not make schooling more democratic; it would merely dilute the right to share in decision-making which those who are genuinely insiders might enjoy by extending it to others who are not. This is a point worth emphasizing. The exponents of participatory democracy are apt to extol the value of people being involved in the government of various institutions which impinge upon their lives.[5] They may be right about this. But it is crucial that their argument not be taken to license a promiscuous approach to the distribution of rights to participate in decision-making. Once that approach is taken, many of the values these writers are anxious to uphold, such as a sense of personal efficacy, will be gravely endangered. If I am a student, the sense of personal efficacy which might accrue through my role in the government of schooling will naturally diminish as the right to participate is extended to more and more people, and the fact that I might be accorded rights to participate in many institutions in which I am less deeply absorbed may be little compensation for the loss.

To be sure, a democratic school is not a sovereign community, and the state within which it exists will rightly oversee its operations with a close eye to the interests of all citizens, and not just the insiders. But it seems altogether probable that the state could discharge its responsibilities in this area while leaving extensive latitude in decision-making to teachers and students. For the sake of the community, for example, the state might impose requirements upon schools with respect to the promotion of morally acceptable attitudes and the teaching of other matters vital to the public interest. For the sake of insiders, the state could adopt practices, such as arbitration boards and the like, to protect the rights of individuals against unjust collective decisions. If the interests of the community, like the rights of individual insiders, can be adequately protected by rather modest external controls upon how schools operate, then I can see no further reason for community involvement; and I can certainly see no reason to champion that cause under the banner of democracy.

It might be objected that I have not done justice to demands for a role in democratic schooling which might be made on behalf of the *local* community. Those who comprise that community could insist that it is their children who attend the school, and the moral significance of that relationship is such that the community cannot be justly viewed as a congeries of outsiders. Now if contact with the children of my neighbourhood is confined to perfunctory encounters of various kinds, it is only sentimentality that could lead me to describe them as my children. In any event, it is clear that relationships as tenuous as this can have no special moral significance. The argument does become a bit more appealing if we interpret it as applying only to those who are deeply involved in the business of child-rearing. In our culture, this class of persons will be virtually coextensive with students' parents. When a parent demands a right to have a voice in decision about the education of her child, we are apt to assume that she is making a weighty moral argument. For example, it is sometimes assumed that when children are taught material at variance with their parents' religion, the *parents'* right to religious liberty is thereby violated.[6] If authoritative decisions within the school often bear as closely as this on parental rights, the parents can hardly be regarded as just concerned outsiders.

The issue of parental rights in education is an extremely difficult one, and I cannot do justice to its complexities in a context where the issue arises as a tangent to my main purpose. I shall briefly make a couple of points, however, which support my position. In the first place, whatever moral rights parents may have in the education of their children, these rights must be circumscribed by the need to safeguard the child's status as an independent, or at least a potentially independent member of the moral community; and I have argued elsewhere that this requirement leads to far weaker parental rights in the area of religious upbringing than we commonly suppose.[7] Parallel arguments can be made about parental rights in other areas of upbringing. A curriculum inappropriate to the educational needs of a particular child, say, or which is designed to ensure fidelity to traditional gender norms could not be justified on the grounds that this is what parents want if their rights were circumscribed in the manner I have indicated.[8] But weak parental rights in educational matters do not appear to be a sound basis for regarding parents as full-fledged insiders, on an equal footing with teachers and students. It is certainly possible, however, that I am wrong about this. Philosophically impressive arguments for stronger parental rights in education than I would countenance have been developed, and these would have to receive very close attention before they could be confidently dismissed.[9] But suppose these arguments turned out to be cogent. It does not follow that my approach is mistaken. On the contrary, *any* credible theory of parental rights will entail that the right to govern the child's life shrinks to vanishing point as the child grows up and becomes capable of taking control of her own life. My discussion of democratic schooling will focus on situations in which a great deal of growing up has already occurred and a substantial capacity to run one's own life has been attained. Therefore, my disregard of parental involvement would make sense even if one accepts a stronger theory of parents' rights than the one I commend.

A brief excursion into the labyrinth of contemporary democratic theory will show that there are two broadly different approaches to justifying democracy, whether it be for the state or some other institution. A democratic regime may be defended on the grounds that it is likely to bring greater success in the pursuit of whatever goals are appropriate to the institution than any feasible alternative.[10] That is to say, authority is supposed to be distributed and regulated in order to produce the maximally competent feasible regime. Therefore, arguments of this kind are derived from what might be called the principle of competence. Alternatively, it may be argued that democratic procedures are intrinsically desirable under certain circumstances, perhaps because authority is bestowed upon those who are morally entitled to it irrespective of competence.[11]

If one were to justify democratic schooling, it may appear that the only viable approach is one that stresses rights at the expense of consequences. Peter Scrimshaw has suggested that people who "give considerable importance" to competence in the government of schooling will "naturally support heads (or teachers as a whole) having major control over educational decisions in schools." On the other hand, where the right to a voice in authoritative decision-making is stressed, a democratic regime is naturally favoured, according to Scrimshaw. The right to a voice in decision-making is supposed to be grounded in the right to freedom which all persons equally share.[12]

Now Scrimshaw pushes his defense of democracy onto very shaky ground by conceding that a concern for competence would favour confining authority to principals and teachers. For even if there were a moral right to freedom with the implications for institutional decision-making which Scrimshaw specifies (and I seriously doubt that there is), the right cannot be reasonably conceived as absolute; and where respecting a merely *prima facie* right would lead to inept decisions about the education of our children, there is surely a powerful case for giving priority to the principle of competence. After all, education is a vitally important business, and a decision to forego the most competent feasible regime is not to be taken lightly.

But what reasons do we have for supposing that the principle of competence will invariably support regimes in which authority is monopolized by teachers or other nonstudents? Two reasons are very widely believed to justify regimes of that kind *via* the principle of competence. It is said that students should not be involved in the government of schooling because they are children, and children cannot be trusted to rule in an intelligent or responsible fashion. Furthermore, there is the position that the wise use of authority in the school depends crucially on academic knowledge which students, regardless of whether they are children or not, necessarily or at least generally lack. Other possible objections to student participation exist, some of which will be examined later on. But I want to deal with these two at the outset because I suspect they are so commonly and deeply held that until they are disposed of, no defence of student participation is likely to be taken seriously. Both objections can be found in two recent books by Colin Wringe, and his presentation of them will provide a suitable starting point for my counterattack. In fairness to Wringe, it should be noted that he does offer some hesitant approval for limited student involvement in decision-making, though what he has in mind appears to be either a right for students to consult with teachers or a right to decide on matters of slight importance.[13] The thrust of his reasoning is emphatically against extending authority to students on any substantial scale.

First of all, Wringe paints a familiar and very unflattering picture of childhood. Children have unstable purposes. What appears important to them now is likely to seem otherwise very shortly; because they have limited experience and weak powers of reasoning, the ends they choose are apt to be trivial and the means injudicious. These alleged characteristics of children make them utterly unqualified for decision-making in any joint enterprise.[14] But Wringe's signally bleak portrait of childhood does not do justice to the immense internal diversity of the student body in contemporary schooling or in any version of that institution we are likely to create in the future. Certainly many students lack any stable purposes, experience of the world or developed powers of reasoning. Yet others have durable and realistic purposes. They are already experienced in making important decisions about their lives and can reason as ably as most adults on matters which bear on their decisions; and we are not at all surprised to find persons who fit this description in the higher grades. Between these two extremes is enormous room for variation, and this intermediate area is doubtless where most of those who attend school (including many teachers and administrators) are to be placed. Wringe's flagrant caricature of childhood cannot justify denying children any substantial voice in the authority structure of schooling, much less the adolescents and young adults who may also be students, precisely because it is a flagrant caricature.

This conclusion might seem to be not altogether fair in light of the distinction Wringe takes from John Kleinig between institutional and normative concepts of childhood.[15] In derogating the capacity of children for responsible decision-making, Wringe uses what he and Kleinig would call normative criteria of childhood. Therefore, the fact that many students may be children only in the institutional sense does not undermine what he says about those who are normatively children. I suggested in chapter four that the distinction between institutional and normative concepts of childhood is just a rather muddled way of marking the difference between childhood and childishness. But I shall not press that point here because even if we accept the distinction, it still does not salvage Wringe's argument.

Wringe is trying to justify the denial of authority not only to students who are normatively children but *also* to those who are not, and he believes that the normative criteria provide the justification. This line of reasoning requires that the normative criteria apply to students without many exceptions. Similarly, one could not be justified in excluding women from positions of authority on grounds of incompetence, unless there were at least a very close fit between womanhood, as a biological category, and normative criteria of femininity which stressed such things as instability, inexperience, and irrationality. Wringe must address the obvious objection that the fit between his normative and institutional criteria is just too loose to support the kind of regime he wants for schools.

Now he does acknowledge that some students will be children only in an institutional sense, but their exclusion from the authority structure is supposedly a price we have to pay because "gerry-mandering and manipulation" are likely in any attempt to assign rights in decision-making directly on the basis of normative criteria.[16] It might be true that who should have rights in decision-making cannot be determined directly according to normative criteria without the likelihood of extensive manipulation and the like in the way the standard is applied. Perhaps determining rights according to age is the least undesirable approach to take here. All this may be granted, but it still does not amount to a persuasive argument for the kind of benevolent despotism Wringe commends. Because the fit between childhood in the institutional and normative senses is going to be decidedly loose in the case of older students, if indeed they count as children in the institutional sense at all, it is plainly reckless to suppose that a concern to protect educational decision-making from the baneful influence of childishness obliges us to favour regimes which exclude older as well as younger students. Of course, the supposition does not look reckless if we believe that Wringe's caricature of childhood is very near the truth even for students who are fast approaching the age of majority. In the case of the latter he does make a grudging concession: "It is ... difficult to see how they can be regarded as totally lacking powers of rational deliberation as they approach these ages."[17] It is difficult indeed. In fact, a child in elementary school totally lacking powers of rational deliberation would surely be a candidate for psychiatric care.

This brings us to the second strand of Wringe's argument which does not advance his position any further than the first. He claims that students are by definition incompetent in matters concerning their education: "To be a pupil ... is precisely to be one who does not fully grasp the nature of the educational goals and standards that are being set before one. Individually and collectively, therefore, pupils are in no position to choose these goals and standards for themselves, nor are they in any position to choose the means and processes by which they are to be achieved, or to judge the competence of those who teach them."[18] A conceptual truth about being a pupil or student may give some specious persuasiveness to this passage. If I were to learn Italian from someone, I would have to defer to my teacher's judgment about the meaning of this or that particular word, what counts as acceptable syntax in Italian, and so on. Without this deference teaching cannot get off the ground. Being a pupil requires trust in the teacher's superior knowledge of what she is to teach, even though this may and perhaps should be a qualified and critical trust; and to that extent, the relationship with the teacher is necessarily "asymmetrical," as Wringe would say. It is altogether possible, however, that my teacher of Italian could turn out to be the most crass philistine, whose grasp of educational goals and standards is far weaker than mine. I might have a much better knowledge of effective methods of language teaching and be better situated to assess her pedagogical competence. All these possibilities are entirely compatible with my *continuing* to be her pupil. Of course, in the world as we know it, educational insight is not always or usually so massively on the side of the student. However, I see no reason to believe that it is must be massively on the side of teachers either.

Wringe adds a puzzling qualification to his second argument which supports a different interpretation than the one I have just considered. He maintains that there are normative and institutional concepts of teacher and pupil which parallel the two sense of childhood he differentiates, and he concedes that the argument applies only to those who are normatively teachers and pupils.[19] I find this puzzling because although we do have evaluative criteria of what it is to be good at teaching or what is a good reason for being a pupil, in no sense do these determine who counts as a teacher or pupil in the first place. According to Wringe, one is a pupil in the normative sense if one is "ignorant of a subject and desires to learn it." This is surely just a reason to become or remain a pupil. Ignorance and the desire to overcome it do not make one a pupil, any more than knowledge and the desire to impart it make one a teacher. But even if Wringe's second argument is conceptually flawed, it could be understood (or reconstructed) as an argument about the kind of regime which befits the school once academically competent teachers are at work.[20] That is to say, the teacher's monopoly on authority might be justified on the grounds of superior academic knowledge, though her superiority would no longer be posited as a conceptual truth. Teachers will almost invariably have the edge over students in the possession of such knowledge (or at least one hopes they will), even if it is worth noting that their advantage should diminish considerably throughout the process of schooling. At any rate, it is widely held that this cognitive advantage justifies a regime dominated by teachers. For instance, Kenneth Strike claims: "The teacher's competence generates the right to govern the intellectually rooted decisions concerning teaching and learning – that is, decisions that require expertise in the concepts of a discipline to make them competently. Included in this category are the selection and organization of the curriculum, the right to direct the process in the classroom in profitable directions, and the right to evaluate the intellectual competence of the student's work."[21] This does not strictly imply that students are to be denied a significant voice in authoritative decision-making since important decisions about teaching and learning might not be intellectually rooted in the stringent sense specified by Strike. However, the context of the passage makes it clear that Strike believes his argument justifies a regime which leaves students out.

What gives Strike's position its substantial *prima facie* appeal is the fact that in *some* of the areas he mentions, decisions patently are intellectually rooted in the relevant sense. It would be irrational to give students the right to direct their own activities in the classroom or to evaluate their own work because competent decisions in either department depend on academic knowledge which students cannot be expected to have. It is easy to assume that those who advocate democratic schooling, or even just substantial student involvement in the government of schooling, are *ipso facto* committed to giving students the right to participate in any and every kind of authoritative decision. The prospect of plebiscites on whether everyone should turn to the next page, give so and so a passing grade, and the like, is not an alluring one, and if these ludicrous practices were required by authority structures which include students, we would certainly be better off with the authoritarian status quo. But there is no such requirement. Even in a highly democratic authority structure, once it is not of the pure participatory variety, specific domains of decision-making can be insulated from direct popular control, and one good reason for doing this is to ensure that decisions which hinge upon specialized knowledge are made in a way which gives due weight to that knowledge. There is a good case for not having the money supply regulated according to direct popular control given a complex economy and expertise on fiscal matters which is not widely diffused. But it does not follow that ordinary citizens should have no voice in government. Likewise, the fact that areas of decision-making within the school are intellectually rooted in Strike's sense is no reason to suppose that students should be entirely excluded from its government. I will grant that teachers should have "the right to direct the process in the classroom in profitable directions, and the right to evaluate the intellectual competence of the student's work." Indeed, where teachers do not have these rights, there is no school, strictly speaking, since schooling requires a social setting where learning is largely directed through teaching and teachers have the right to exercise direction. Schooling is logically incompatible with pure participatory democracy, but the fact that it is does nothing to justify authority structures which leave students out. We can continue to have schools and acknowledge the fact that some decisions about the education of our children are intellectually rooted, and therefore must belong to teachers. Nevertheless, we may opt for any of a large range of authority structures which could properly be described as democratic or quasi-democratic.

It would no doubt be imprudent to take any such option if virtually all authoritative decisions within schooling were intellectually rooted in Strike's sense. Strike evidently assumes that they are, but that is a mistake. A highly inclusive category of important decisions within the school are at best tenuously connected with "expertise in the concepts of a discipline." Consider teachers' alleged rights in the selection and organization of the curriculum. In some matters here reason obliges us to defer to the academic expert. The logical grammar of disciplines places some constraints on how any curriculum is to be organized, but these constraints still leave us with enormous discretion in deciding what is to be learnt and how it is to be learnt.[22] The academic accomplishments of teachers, however great they might be, are not sufficient to justify any exclusive claim to authority in matters of curriculum. If an adolescent were deeply interested in history, say, and wanted to forego the study of physics in order to give a freer rein to her interests, then why would the teacher's expertise in physics (or any other academic discipline for that matter) generate the right to decide whether or not the student's curriculum is to include physics? It is not obvious that cases of this kind would be dealt with competently under democratic regimes. That remains to be seen. However, it is obvious that the possession of academic expertise does not itself generate any exclusive rights for teachers to decide in matters like these because these are not, at least in any familiar sense, purely academic decisions. Of course, one might adopt a conception of education which emphasizes the value of breadth of knowledge, irrespective of students' interests, and then go on to argue that teachers would be more likely to make decisions about the curriculum which consort with that conception. But that position is at best highly contestable, and besides, it is not Strike's. He does develop an intriguing analogy between the kind of authority structure he believes befits an academic discipline and the kind of undemocratic regime which is supposedly proper for the school.[23] But the analogy begs rather than answers the crucial question here. One needs to know *why* schools and academic disciples should be conceived of as analogous with respect to the distribution of authority, and the analogy itself can provide no answer.

The difficulties of Strike's approach do not end with the issue of curriculum control. Consider the role of academic knowledge in decisions about how social order is to be maintained in the school. Those who make such decisions could certainly benefit from some systematic reflection on the nature and point of discipline and punishment, and philosophy will be helpful in doing this. Psychology and sociology might also have a useful contribution to make. But these facts cannot bear the weight which Strike's argument would place upon them. In the first place, it is surely the case that competent decisions are constantly being made in schools about discipline and punishment without any systematic reflection on their nature and point, much less systematic reflection which draws upon philosophy, psychology, and sociology. More important, the academic knowledge which is likely to be of real use here will not be especially sophisticated; and for that reason it will be as intellectually accessible to most older students as it is to most teachers. We can hardly be troubled if those who exercise authority in this area have not mastered all the nuances of Herbert Hart's theory of punishment or if they cannot assess the scholarship of Michel Foucault's *Discipline and Punish*. It is only through a wildly generous use of the term "expertise" that one could claim that competent decisions about discipline and punishment require academic expertise or are even substantially facilitated by its possession. The same point can be made about many other areas of decision-making, even those where considerations pertaining to academic knowledge figure prominently. Competent decisions about the hiring of teachers depend upon a just estimate of the candidates' knowledge of the subjects they will teach, but in the ordinary course of events a perusal of academic references and university transcripts will suffice. The competent decision-maker does not have to be an expert or even someone moderately knowledgeable in the relevant subjects.

I do not wish to suggest that authority should be confined to teachers only where decisions are intellectually rooted. In practice this is hardly going to be feasible. Many decisions about the curriculum and its implementation, say, might be made according to democratic procedures while preserving the pedagogical rights essential to the idea of schooling. But even so, democratization might still be pushed to an extent that destroys the initiative and commitment of teachers. One can imagine a situation in which elected committees devise minute regulations about the pace and sequence of instruction, the methods to be used, and so forth. Teachers would still have to make authoritative decisions when applying these regulations within the classroom and therefore they would have the right, albeit a closely circumscribed and tenuous right, to direct the learning of their students. Nevertheless, the individual teacher would be so pervasively hemmed in by the authority of the group that her right to teach would seem virtually worthless – in these circumstances, we surely cannot expect good teaching. For similar reasons, completely divorcing the practice of discipline from the role of teachers is not an attractive policy. Dearden's facetious suggestion that we have "bouncers" in the classroom to enforce discipline while teachers occupy themselves exclusively with academic matters is intended to illustrate a conceptual possibility;[24] it could hardly be construed as a sensible practical recommendation. Good teaching can only be expected if we give teachers a good deal of elbow room in the way they use authority within the classroom, and the room they need will certainly go beyond what could be justified solely in terms of their academic expertise. But this fact furnishes no grounds for undemocratic schooling. It is often argued that elected representatives within democratic states, and even professional civil servants, should have more than a little latitude in the way they perform their roles, but whatever force these arguments might have, they do not show that democratic states are undesirable. In the case of schooling, as in the case of the state, the room to manoevre which has to be built into certain roles in order to maintain morale and encourage imagination is hardly so great that democracy is precluded. Many fields of authority within the school might involve extensive student participation without encroaching destructively upon the practice of teaching – the making of disciplinary decisions outside the classroom, the design of a code of conduct, even hiring and firing. I will gladly grant that if student participation is incompetent in these areas then the quality of teaching is bound to suffer. But we have yet to find any persuasive grounds for supposing that their participation would be incompetent.

My objectives in this section of the chapter have been modest. I have pointed out that whatever the connection between being a student and being childish, it is not strong enough to justify regimes dominated by non-students. I have argued that there is an ample range of authoritative decisions within the ambit of schooling not deeply rooted in academic expertise. Finally, I tried to show that there is no apparent incompatibility between regimes which give teachers the substantial range of authority which good teaching requires and the demands of democracy. All this is a far cry from a defence of student participation in the government of schooling, much less a defence strong enough to support anything close to democratic rule. It is to this more ambitious task that I shall now turn.

Whatever one's conception of education may be, if it is at all defensible it must entail that the learning which makes persons educated comes to be appreciated by such persons. That is to say, to be educated is in part to understand and *prize* what is in one's educational interest. If poetry is educational and pushpin is not, then the educated person will not only understand that this is so; she will also value what is educational, and for that reason be inclined to choose it in appropriate circumstances. The moral necessity of this point is not hard to discern. If we were to say that education has achieved all that is necessary and desirable once an individual has mastered a certain quantum of learning, regardless of whether or not she appreciates what she has mastered, we would be guilty of grievous disrespect for persons; we would be implying that the learner's subjective viewpoint is of no consequence whatever at any stage of the educational process and we would be treating her merely as a resource to be used for the sake of values which need never become her own. The importance of this point is not just morally incontestable – it is also widely acknowledged by a diverse range of educational writers from Illich and Freire to Oakshott and Peters.

A further point will be central to the ensuing argument. The qualities of mind which characterize the educated person are not extrinsic ends of educational processes but rather achievements which have to be progressively realized *within* the various processes. Educated persons are not the outcome of some psychological metamorphosis which one undergoes when certain activities of learning have terminated; they are rather beings who gradually take shape while engaging in such activities. It does not follow that everything which counts as an educational process will instantiate the end towards which it is directed. As Peters has noted, the fact that a developed interest in science is part of one's educatedness does not mean that engagement in every process which contributed to that outcome necessarily manifested some degree of scientific interest.[25] My point is simply that educational ends and processes cannot be separated so neatly that a developed interest in science, say, could reasonably be conceived as the outcome of processes in which interest was not progressively engendered. Perhaps some intelligible beings do become educated persons through processes in which the ends are not intimated and gradually realized – processes analogous to what leads to a caterpillar's transformation into a butterfly, for example – but these would patently not be *human* beings. Again, I would emphasize that my point does not presuppose the desirability of any particular conception of education. What I have just said about the interpenetration of educational ends and processes is consistent with any number of radically different views about the ends of educations and the means by which they should be pursued.

I have suggested that on any plausible conception of education, becoming educated crucially involves coming to appreciate what is one's educational interest. Given the interpenetration of educational achievements and processes, this particular achievement will gradually crystallize within the process of becoming educated. Now I assume that in an educationally adequate form of schooling, students will leave, as a rule, having attained a substantial level of success with respect to the central ends of education, even if we would not describe most of them as highly educated persons. This is hardly an exacting standard of adequacy, and it is important for my argument that it not be exacting. An educationally adequate form of schooling, in the sense I have stipulated, should not be an unrealistic aspiration for even moderately prosperous societies. It must be the case, then, that in a schooling system which meets my standard, students are likely to be at least quite close to having a sound appreciation of what is in their educational interest during the latter years of attendance. In that event, it is reasonable to suppose that they can be trusted to decide competently on some important matters concerning their own education.[26]

Yet it does not strictly follow that we have good reasons to trust students with a voice within the government of schooling. After all, a decision about one's education is not necessarily an authoritative decision. It is easy to envisage schools in which attendance at classes is voluntary, students enjoy extensive room for choice in what they study, for example, while at the same time the *right* to devise and enforce regulational about attendance, curricular choice, and so on, lies exclusively in the hands of teachers. Indeed, conditions of the kind I have described are familiar in some contemporary secondary schools and universities. But if students can be trusted to make some important decisions about their own education, why can they not be trusted to perform competently within the government of schooling? There is an anomaly here in the position of those who want to drawn the line against student participation. It is incumbent on them to show that some special features of *authoritative* decision-making in schooling are such that student participation is or is likely to be incompetent, even in the circumstances I am considering. A number of considerations might be used to attempt to show this, but none I can imagine carries much weight.

Authoritative decisions within the school oblige one to consider the normative interests of others, indeed many others, and so ideally, decisions will be strictly impartial with regard to those who may benefit or suffer from what is decided. The importance of impartiality in this connection gives a moral dimension to the exercise of authority, and would seem to make moral maturity an important standard when deciding who is competent to exercise it. If teachers are likely to demonstrate a much higher level of moral maturity than students, then there would certainly be compelling grounds for confining authority to teachers. Further, the competent exercise of authority in any social setting requires an understanding of how possible decisions are likely to reverberate through the setting and beyond, as well as an ability to bring that understanding to bear in making choices. A.S. Carson has emphasized the alleged superiority of teachers in such understanding and ability in his argument for placing control of the curriculum exclusively in the hands of teachers.[27] Others have also made the point that the inevitable brevity of student participation in the authority structure under the conditions I am considering would lead to a serious loss of competence. Antony Flew has made this objection to student participation at the university level.[28] I shall consider each objection in turn.

First, we should bear in mind that if teachers do in fact demonstrate a *much* higher level of moral maturity than students at the latter stages of schooling – and it is very far from obvious that they do – it follows that we are failing in the job of moral education. A disparity in moral maturity of that order would not be reason for being hesitant to include students in the authority structure; it would rather be cause for alarm about our failure to provide a satisfactory education in at least one crucial area. Insofar as we overcame our failure in moral education, the argument for excluding students from the authority structure on moral grounds would correspondingly weaken.

It is certainly possible, perhaps even likely, that even when a substantial level of success in moral education is achieved, there would still be some nontrivial difference in moral maturity between students in their years immediately prior to graduation and teachers. But it is extremely doubtful that whatever difference might persist could yield strong grounds for a regime dominated by teachers. This is because under regimes which involve extensive popular participation, the need to ensure that those in authority satisfy stringent criteria of moral excellence is far less pressing than it is under rival authority structures. For example, in arguing for democratic states or workplace-democracy for adults, we do not ordinarily assume that each individual will choose with exemplary impartiality. That would be unrealistic. We expect self-interest to be a prominent factor in determining how most individuals vote, and we are not surprised enough to be disappointed when elected representatives fail to show a saintly disinterestedness. The impartiality which is morally desirable is approximated, however, because in democratic voting procedures the voice of each participant carries equal weight and elected representatives are periodically selected or rejected according to procedures of that kind. I will grant that where extreme moral weakness is rampant we cannot expect that popular participation within an authority structure will lead to anything tolerably close to impartial rule. For one thing, the risk of majority tyranny will be dangerously high. But that is not the kind of situation I am considering. My point is simply that if we are doing a fairly decent job of moral education, it cannot be reasonably assumed that the moral deficiencies of students could typically be so great that all authority structures should be ruled out which give them a significant voice.

This takes us to the objection that authority should be confined to teachers because of their detailed understanding of the specific context of decision-making and their ability to apply that knowledge in making wise choices. Now it can hardly be denied that students during the latter years of schooling have become acquainted with the institutional context in which they have participated for several years. Those who have arrived at the school very recently will not be familiar with its unique features, but in this respect they are no different from recently hired teachers or administrators and they will certainly be familiar with similar institutions. It would be utterly shocking if students in secondary schools were typically incapable of making any sensible predictions about the effects of firing a gifted but iconoclastic teacher or hiring an autocratic principal, or introducing a new disciplinary code, and equally shocking if they had no sense of the weight to be attached to such effects in practical deliberation. But even if students are not utterly ignorant in this area, it does seem likely that in current circumstances teachers are apt to be rather less ignorant, and rather more able to use their knowledge in decision-making.

However, if there is a large disparity in knowledge and ability between teachers and students, it seems probable that much of it could be explained away in a manner which makes the advantage of teachers largely irrelevant to the justification of regimes which leave students out.

For obvious reasons, understanding the likely effects of various possible authoritative decisions in a given institutional setting and being able to apply that understanding in practice are encouraged and developed by the opportunity to make such decisions. Admittedly, some individuals fail to progress despite the opportunity to make decisions, but that does not affect the point at issue. The denial of any significant voice in the authority structure of an institution deprives one of a potent incentive to reflect seriously upon the merits and demerits of the various options available to those in authority. For if what one thinks about the options carries no weight in the decision-making process itself, there is little point to reflection. It is still possible to reflect upon the process with a spectator's fascination, but in the absence of that rather untypical human interest, an individual might as well turn her attention to other matters and just hope that those in authority will do a good job. When that course is taken, learning about the institutional context of decision-making will certainly grind to a halt. It is small wonder that widespread political apathy and naïveté often characterize authoritarian states or mass democracies in which the individual vote counts for next to nothing.[29]

In contemporary schooling teachers are deeply involved in the exercise of authority, even in situations where the same thing can be said of the state or parents. Their involvement gives a point to serious reflection on the practical context of decision-making, and it is not surprising then that conscientious and intelligent teachers will quickly develop a shrewd sense of the likely consequences of possible decisions and of how that knowledge is to be used. If students lag far behind teachers in this area of their development, even during the last years of attendance, that is entirely predictable given their exclusion from the authority structure. Moreover, if students were accorded the opportunity to participate, this would be a potent incentive for them to learn about the context of that process, and the current disparity between teachers and students with respect to their understanding of decision-making would naturally diminish.

The objection remains that students cannot be expected to use authority competently because of their short-lived role within the government of schooling. This is one of Flew's objections, and be cause, apart from a brief allusion to the value of efficiency, he does not explain his grounds for pressing it.[30] I am obliged to speculate about what these grounds would be. It might be suggested that any regime which gave a significant voice to students would not adequately safeguard the normative interests of future students. Perhaps students would have little reason to reject policies which might have damaging effects in the future if they will not be around to suffer the consequences. Further, giving authority to students could be though destructive of efficiency either because an inevitably brief period of participation leaves them little time for learning about the institutional context of decision-making, even if participation is the potent incentive to learn which I have said it is, or because frequent changes in the composition of the authority structure would produce frequent discontinuities in the making and implementing of policies.

In order to show that regimes involving students would seriously threaten the interests of their successors, given the conditions I have been considering, it is necessary to establish that serious conflicts of interest are likely to arise between those who are engaged in the authority structure at a particular time and those who will attend school later on. What I have been looking at is the possibility of extending authority to students in situations where they are likely to have an approximately sound appreciation of what is in their educational interest, are at a decent level of moral maturity, and can exercise authority with some sensitivity to the institutional context in which they operate; what *these* students decide cannot be expected to endanger the interests of those who come afterwards unless serious conflicts of interest occur. But precisely where are these conflicts supposed to arise? If a new teacher is to be hired, say, or a disciplinary code is to be revised, it will surely be only in very unusual circumstances that a substantial divergence will occur between what is best for students who are currently in school and those who will attend in the future. Moreover, decisions which turn out badly for future students can ordinarily be reversed without significant costs when their time comes to make decisions – teachers who are incompetent can be dismissed, disciplinary codes can be revised to suit present needs, and so on.

The suggestion that brevity of participation disables students from learning enough about the institutional context of decision-making does carry some weight, but rather less than would initially appear. First, provisions can be made to encourage this kind of learning to some extent, even before the powerful incentive of actual involvement in government is brought into play. In fact, teachers who respect the burgeoning critical capacities of their students already do this at the elementary level. The pros and cons of specific rules can be discussed, the point of this or that act of punishment can be explained, some authoritative decisions can be negotiated. Of course, this process can be pushed to absurd extremes. If every authoritative act is to be subjected to meticulous discussion, explanation, or negotiation, opportunity to learn about anything else would be negligible. However, it is surely obvious that without going to such lengths it is possible to bring children to some substantial appreciation of the practical context of exercising authority *before* they are put in a position to do so. Perhaps the level of success which is generally feasible here would not be enough to warrant fully democratic regimes, even at the latter stages of schooling, but it seems absurd to suppose that so little success is feasible, that all regimes which involve students to a significant degree are doomed to incompetence.

The claim that brevity of participation would militate against efficiency by generating frequent changes in policy, and so on, can be dismissed rather easily. Efficiency is a matter of maximizing success in some undertaking while minimizing the expenditure of resources. From the viewpoint of efficiency, the fact that particular policies are continued or discontinued is of no intrinsic concern at all – everything depends on whether what is abandoned or taken up is efficient or inefficient. Indeed, given that there are appropriate changes in goals over time and also changes in available resources, a concern for efficiency will certainly lead to changes in policy to meet the criteria of efficiency.

I have tried to show that in a schooling system which satisfies a quite modest standard of educational adequacy, it is reasonable to trust students with some important decisions about their own education. Various objections to extending this trust into the sphere of authority have been shown to carry little or no force. This amounts to a *prima facie* case for student participation in the government of schooling. Still, it is not certain that the principle of competence would often favour regimes which include students to a significant extent, even in conditions of educational adequacy. In those conditions it does not appear that student participation would be downright incompetent, although we might still have reason to believe that an authority structure dominated by teachers (of the right kind) would be a bit more successful. In particular, the possibility remains that even when students can govern well, time and energy devoted to that end would detract from educational purposes. Dunlop stresses this point in a rather extravagant manner. "All experience shows that if there is to be discussion of everything that affects people, an enormous amount of time has to be set aside for meetings. How schools could ever find time for this extra claim for timetable space (even if it were thought worth while) altogether escapes me."[31] It altogether escapes me as well. But our agreement about this is beside the point because no one in their right mind could ever advocate an authority structure for schooling, or any other institution for that matter, in which "everything that affects people" is determined through collective choice. Nevertheless, there is a serious argument here. If student participation in the government of schooling is just an interruption in their education, then this will count against their participation if we want a regime which conduces to maximum educational success. The objection can be parried only if it is shown that political participation has, or is at least likely to have, educational benefits in the kind of context I am considering. I believe I can show this.

The last stage of my argument relies heavily on an interpretation of Aristotle's theory of how the development of virtues, in the broad sense of excellent features of character, is tied to their exercise. In the *Nicomachean Ethics*, Aristotle presents the theory in a manner which gives it a deceptively paradoxical look. "The virtues we get by first exercising them, as also happens in the case of the arts as well. For the things we have to learn before we can do them we learn by doing them, e.g. men become builders by building and lyre-players by playing the lyre; so too we become just by doing just acts, temperate by doing temperate acts, brave by doing brave acts."[32] The virtues are acquired by practising them. But how can we practise what we do not already have? The appearance of incoherence is dissipated once it is acknowledged that virtues, like other educational ends, are intimated and gradually realized within the processes through which we pursue them. I emphasized this point in the previous section, but it is worth illustrating how it applies in the present context. A child's first displays of kindness, say, only faintly resemble the benevolence of our moral saints or heroes, just as her first attempts to play the violin are only crudely similar to the performances of virtuosi. In neither case does the view that practice is the route to success presuppose that what is pursued has already been attained. But in each case, the modest achievements of the neophyte foreshadow the excellence of character or skill to which her efforts may lead; and without these achievements, and the practice which makes them progressively better, the perfection of character and skill would never occur.

Aristotle's comparison between the learning of virtues and the learning of arts is illuminating, and not just because it highlights the fact, which is quite obvious anyhow, that an element of habituation is essential to moral education. Rather more interesting is the light he throws on the connection between the exercise of virtue and the development of understanding and proficiencies intrinsic to moral excellence. The performance of an accomplished violinist, for example, involves myriad and highly subtle motor discriminations which draw upon a rich understanding of the instrument's musical possibilities. The violinist's motor facility and the understanding it reflects depend highly upon practice. Likewise, Aristotle would argue that the practice of the virtues in their developed forms requires one consistently to discriminate and choose a mean that is finely poised between opposing vices. The proficiencies and understanding which make this achievement possible are encapsulated in Aristotle's obscure concept of "practical wisdom,"[33] and I take it that part of the point of assimilating learning the arts to learning the virtues is to underscore the vital role of practice in perfecting this so-called practical wisdom. It is true that Aristotle includes the latter among the intellectual virtues and says that these "in the main" owe their growth to teaching rather than habituation,[34] but it does not follow that he regarded practice as unimportant in the cultivation of the cognitive component of moral excellence.[35] Anyhow, I am less interested here in Aristotelian exegesis than in discerning what significance his comparison might have to our understanding of the development of character.

In order to appreciate what I take to be the essential insight in Aristotle's comparison, it is not strictly necessary to accept the doctrine of the mean. Whatever can be said for or against that doctrine, the development of any virtue clearly involves ever-increasing powers of discrimination and understanding, powers highly contingent upon practice. A toddler is able to identify the giving of a gift or the sharing of toys as an act of kindness, but at an even slightly more sophisticated level the difference between virtuous action and the manifestation of other states of character completely eludes her. Without the determined exercise of virtue, one remains arrested at something close to this infantile level of moral myopia. Selfishness is confused with standing up for one's own rights, vanity or recklessness with courage, arrogance with self-respect, and so forth. Certainly moments of penetrating moral insight are possible in a life devoted to depravity. But I take it that Aristotle's point is (or should be) that attaining and *sustaining* the powers of moral discernment intrinsic to excellence of character, as opposed to exhibiting a fitful perspicacity, are not possible without the discipline of practice. For parallel reasons we might expect flashes of brilliance in the performance of a musically gifted person who is using a difficult instrument she scarcely ever plays, but a consistently accomplished performance would be little short of miraculous.

It may be worth noting here that the view I have been describing is not reducible to any conceptual truth about the connection between the exercise and development of virtue. It is just conceivable that one might become a paragon of temperance or benevolence through processes which did not involve the exercise of those virtues to any significant extent. But the bare conceptual possibility of this being so is no more interesting than the fact that one might become a violin virtuoso by watching Itzhak Perlman play or by undergoing brain surgery. Aristotle's theory is intended to fit the facts about becoming virtuous in the world as we know it rather than whatever might be true in all possible worlds.

I would suggest that Aristotle's theory can be reasonably thought to hold in the case of the development of autonomy. Autonomy is an excellence of character – a virtue in the Aristotelian sense. In its developed form it demands refined powers of discernment and understanding. For one thing, an individual must have an acute sensitivity to the human proclivity for self-deception if control of her life is not to be lost. The deepest psychological interests have to be clearly seen for what they are in the context of framing the will, or self-rule will be subverted through the pull of temptation. The analysis of autonomy offered in chapter two should make it very clear that this is no "easy virtue", requiring little of our mental abilities. That is the point of calling it an ideal. Perhaps the exercise of the relevant powers has to be largely tacit and spontaneous, like the application of musical skills in a virtuosic performance, but in neither case does it make much sense to suppose that development could proceed far without extensive opportunities to exercise these powers.

If the development and exercise of autonomy are connected in this manner, then a schooling system devoted to the end of cultivating autonomy must be concerned with ensuring, among other things, ample scope for its exercise. This certainly does not entail that we should have democratic schooling, but it does support the proposal that other things being equal we should favour authority structures which give students maximum scope for the exercise of autonomy. In accepting that proposal, one is not implicitly abandoning or qualifying the principle of competence; on the contrary, it is difficult to see how one could reject the proposal if one accepts the principle and also maintains that schooling should be centrally concerned with encouraging autonomy.

I believe that the force of this point becomes apparent if we see it in the context of a certain tradition in western democratic theory, a tradition ably represented by Carole Pateman's *Participation and Democratic Theory*. Pateman argues for a "participatory society," one in which individuals are able to participate in the authority structures of virtually all the associations with which they are concerned.[36] She offers a particular reading of how the principle of competence applies in the evaluation of authority structures, given her interpretation of the principle of competence. According to that principle, authority should be distributed and regulated to ensure that it will be exercised in the best feasible manner. In applying the principle to states, for example, one will obviously ask about the quality of decisions likely to be made under different constitutions. Will extensive popular participation conduce to inefficiency? And if so to what extent will it do so? Will the centralization of authority give rise to the havoc of utopian social engineering? These are questions about the legislative consequences of different political orders, and the questions of this kind are certainly relevant to the principle of competence. But Pateman's crucial point, as I understand it, is that questions of this kind are not the only ones relevant to the application of that principle. Suppose we have to make a choice between two political regimes, X and Y. With respect to the quality of decision-making, X has a slight edge – there is likely to be greater efficiency, and so forth. But suppose X, unlike Y, is a regime in which authority is confined to a tiny, skilled, and benevolent elite. It might be the case that this authority structure would have deleterious consequences for the characters of those subject to its decisions. It might have corrosive effects upon their sense of personal efficacy, their community spirit, and so on, irrespective of how competently the elite govern. If we believe with Pateman that the primary purpose of government is to develop the virtue and intelligence of the citizenry,[37] there would be good reason, given that we want maximum success in the pursuit of that purpose, to opt for Y, despite the sacrifice of efficiency and the like which would be involved. Surprisingly, her principle of competence would not favour confining authority to those who are most accomplished at decision-making.

I am not interested here in defending the participatory society Pateman envisions. I do want to emphasize, however, that her argument does reveal something important about how the principle of competence would apply to a schooling system which has the primary purpose of developing student's autonomy. Suppose we are choosing between two possible authority structures for the latter stages of schooling, and we are choosing for a system which meets the conditions of educational adequacy I specified earlier on. One of the structures is democratic or quasi-democratic. The other excludes students from any significant role. Under the latter regime, the quality of decision-making is a bit higher: resources are managed more prudently, the right curricular policies are more likely to be adopted, and so on. These facts favour the regime which leaves students out, according to the principle of competence, but they do not yield a decisive argument in favour of that regime. For it is *also* important to consider the fact that an authority structure which excludes students denies them important opportunities to exercise and thereby develop their autonomy. This fact is especially important because under conditions of educational adequacy it seems unreasonable to suppose, in light of the arguments I marshalled earlier on in the chapter, that there could be a great disparity between teachers and students with respect to the quality of authoritative decision-making in the latter years.

One last point I would like to consider is not so much an objection to my argument as an attempt to deflect any force it might have in the criticism of current practices in our schools. I have presented an argument which applies under conditions of educational adequacy. It is certain to be objected that those conditions do not now prevail. The students who populate our secondary schools, as a rule, are nowhere near a secure appreciation of what is in their educational interest and are utterly ill-prepared to make authoritative decisions in a manner that would enhance the development of autonomy. After several years of schooling, so little light has penetrated their benighted minds that they still cannot be trusted with any authority. This takes us back to something like Wringe's bleak portrait of childhood, and I have already indicated quite emphatically what I think about that. But suppose I am mistaken. After all, the truth is sometimes very shocking and counterintuitive.

If the education of the students in our secondary schools has progressed so little after such prolonged attendance, it is important to ask why this is so. Whichever answer the question receives, it will clearly create very serious difficulties for anyone who wants to press the objection that my argument is irrelevant under current conditions. Suppose this educational failure is due to deficiencies in the way we bring up our children. Poor teaching is rampant inside the classroom, perhaps, and powerful anti-educational forces are at work outside it. So long as these deficiencies persist, we have not only culpably failed to provide the kind of education we should provide; we have brought into doubt the very justification of schooling. The point of authority is to bring success to some worthwhile social undertaking, and I take it that for schooling the relevant success is educational. If protracted and costly effort on the part of teachers and pupils brings so little success, then there is little point either to their efforts or to the authority structure of schooling itself. One cannot elude this difficulty by supposing that the alleged fecklessness of students, their inability to appreciate their normative interests, and so on, are due to the *nature* of childhood and adolescence, rather than any deficiencies in the way we bring them up. Beings who are barely educable are surely best left in that condition, at least until they reach an age at which they become more amenable to the influence of civilization, because our most strenuous efforts to overcome their "natural" vices will be largely doomed to failure.

In short, though my argument pertains to conditions which might not be found in contemporary schooling, that can bring little consolation to whoever believes that demands for student involvement in government need not be taken seriously. For if those conditions do not prevail, the justification of contemporary schooling on educational grounds would be in grave doubt.

Notes

INTRODUCTION

1 R.F. Dearden, *The Philosophy of Primary Education* (London: Routledge & Kegan Paul 1968); P.H. Hirst and R.S. Peters, *The Logic of Education* (London: Routledge & Kegan Paul 1970).
2 R.S. Peters, *Essays on Educators* (London: Allen & Unwin 1981).
3 Hirst and Peters, *The Logic of Education*, 36-9.
4 In fact, I have argued that Dewey's liberalism is thoroughly superficial. See "Education for Democracy: John Dewey's Illiberal Philosophy of Education," *Educational Theory* 32, no. 2 (1982): 167-76. The same charge is often made against Rousseau, though I think it is less defensible in that context.
5 Eamonn Callan, "Indoctrination and Parental Rights," in *Philosophy of Education 1985: Proceedings of the Forty-First Annual Meeting*, ed. David Nyberg (Normal, Illinois: Philosophy of Education Society 1985), 97-106; and Eamonn Callan, "McLaughlin on Parental Rights," *Journal of Philosophy of Education* 19, no. 2 (1985): 111-18.

CHAPTER ONE

1 See, for example, Charles Bailey, *Beyond the Present and Particular* (London: Routledge & Kegan Paul 1984), 20-2.
2 For example, A.S. Neill, *Summerhill* (New York: Hart Publishing Co. 1960).
3 Isaiah Berlin, *Four Essays on Liberty* (Oxford: Oxford University Press 1969), 118-72.
4 Ibid., 122-34.
5 Quoted in Felix Oppenheim, *Dimensions of Freedom* (New York: St Martin's Press 1961), 177.

6   John Dewey, *Experience and Education* (New York: Collier Books 1963), 61.
7   This claim is a commonplace in recent philosophical literature. A scholarly and highly influential defence can be found in Gerald C. McCallum, "Negative and Positive Freedom," *Philosophical Review* 76, no. 2 (1967): 312-44.
8   S.I. Benn and R.S. Peters, *Social Principles and the Democratic State* (London: Allen & Unwin 1959), 249; Oppenheim, *Dimensions of Freedom*, 67-89; William Parent, "Some Recent Work on the Concept of Liberty," *American Philosophical Quarterly* 11, no. 3 (1974): 149-67.
9   Quoted in Oppenheim, *Dimensions of Freedom*, 120.
10 See P.H. Partridge, "Freedom," in *The Encyclopedia of Philosophy*, 8 vols. ed. Paul Edwards (New York: Macmillan Publishing Co. 1967), 3:222.
11 Parent, "Some Recent Work on the Concept of Liberty," 154; John Hospers, *Libertarianism* (Los Angeles: Nash Publishing 1971), 10-12.
12 Berlin, *Four Essays on Liberty*, liv.
13 What is now usually dubbed "libertarianism" is based upon the assumption that freedom is supremely important in political decisions. However, its exponents are usually oblivious to the fact that what they call "liberty" is worthless without the ability to avail oneself of one's options. See Robert Nozick, *Anarchy, State, and Utopia* (New York: Basic Books 1974); and Hospers, *Libertarianism*. For a very different variety of libertarianism, which depends on a criterion of constraint not dissimilar from the one I suggest, see Lawrence Crocker's masterly study, *Positive Liberty* (The Hague: Martinus Nijhoff 1980).
14 Joel Feinberg, *Rights, Justice, and the Bounds of Liberty* (Princeton: Princeton University Press 1980), 36.
15 J.S. Mill, *On Liberty* (Indianapolis: The Bobbs-Merrill Company 1976), 19-90.
16 Vinit Haksar, *Equality, Liberty and Perfectionism* (Oxford: Oxford University Press 1979), 172-84.
17 Ronald Dworkin, *Taking Rights Seriously* (Cambridge, Mass.: Harvard University Press 1978), 201-2.
18 Feinberg, *Rights, Justice, and the Bounds of Liberty*, 36-43.
19 The example is adapted from Ronald Dworkin's argument against the existence of any right to liberty (as opposed to specific liberties). See Dworkin, *Taking Rights Seriously*, 266-72.
20 The idea that the value of freedom might be explained in this way has been briefly defended by Gerald Dworkin. But I am not certain that he is talking about what I would call "autonomy," and if he is, I do not think he would approve of some of the detailed points I make about the connection between autonomy and freedom. See Gerald Dworkin, "Is

More Choice Better than Less?", in *Midwest Studies in Philosophy*, ed. Peter A. French, Theodore E. Uehling Jr., and Howard K. Wettstein (Minneapolis: University of Minnesota Press 1982), 7:47-61.

CHAPTER TWO

1 R.F. Dearden, "Autonomy and Education," in *Education and Reason*, ed. R.F. Dearden, P.H. Hirst and R.S. Peters (London: Routledge & Kegal Paul 1975), 63.
2 In connecting personal autonomy with the idea of a motivational structure I have been strongly influenced by Michael Bonnett's fine paper, "Authenticity, Autonomy and Compulsory Curriculum," *Cambridge Journal of Education* 6, no. 3 (1976): 107-21.
3 Aristotle, *Nicomachean Ethics*, trans. David Ross (Oxford: Oxford University Press 1980), 1103a14-b25.
4 Charles Taylor, "Responsibility for Self," in *The Identities of Persons*, ed. Amelie O. Rorty (Berkeley and Los Angeles: University of California Press 1976), 282.
5 The cnnection between interest and intrinsic evaluation is brought out in P.S. Wilson, *Interest and Discipline in Education* (London: Routledge & Kegan Paul 1971), 66.
6 Cf. John Dewey, *Democracy and Education* (New York: Macmillan 1916), 137; and A.R. White, "Dewey's Theory of Interest," in *John Dewey Reconsidered*, ed. R.S. Peters (London: Routledge & Kegan Paul 1977), 50-3.
7 Ralmond Gaita, "Integrity," *Proceedings of the Aristotelian Society*, supplementary vol. 55 (1981): 161-76. Realism is not the same as what Gaita calls "integrity." His opening example makes it clear that people can evince the spirit of truthfulness in heroic measure but be incapable of bringing it to bear in shaping their own lives.
8 For example, S.I. Benn, "Freedom, Autonomy and the Concept of a Person," *Proceedings of the Aristotelian Society* 76 (1976): 124-8. Benn does concede that continuous ratiocination is neither necessary nor desirable but he defines the autonomous person as someone whose beliefs, principles, and values are "the outcome of a still-continuing process of criticism and re-evaluation" (124). A similar emphasis can be found in R.F. Dearden's writings on the subject of autonomy. See R.F. Dearden, "Autonomy and Education," 58-75; in *Philosophers Discuss Education*, ed. S.C. Brown (London: Macmillan 1970), 3-18.
9 David Riesman, *The Lonely Crowd* (New Haven: Yale University Press 1950), 11-12.
10 See H.H. Price, "Belief and Will," in R.F. Dearden, P.H. Hirst and R.S. Peters *Reason*, ed. (London: Routledge & Kegan Paul 1975), 198-217.

11 Iris Murdoch, *The Soveignty of Good* (London: Routledge & Kegan Paul 1970), 83–4.

12 For example, Benjamin Gibbs, Autonomy and Authority in Education," *Journal of Philosophy of Education* 13 (1979): 122.

13 For example, P.H. Nowell-Smith, *Ethics* (Harmondsworth: Penguin Books 1954), 319–20; C.D. Hardie, *Truth and Fallacy in Educational Theory* (New York: Teacher's College Press 1962), 126–7; R.S. Peters, "Was Plato Nearly Right about Education?" , ed. R.S. Peters (London: Allend & Unwin 1981), 29–31.

14 J.P. White, *The Aims of Education Restated* (London: Routledge & Kegan Paul 1982), 51.

15 The appeal of rule-utilitarianism stems from its supposed ability to support those widely and deeply held moral principles which have nothing explicitly to do with the maximization of happiness or satisfaction. At the same time, it allegedly provides these principles with a unifying rationale and a way of adjudicating between them when they come into conflict. See R.M. Hare, *Moral Thinking* (Oxford: Oxford University Press 1981). Although Hare believes that rule-utilitarianism can be justified without appealing to substantive moral intuitions, he is anxious to meet the charge of counterintuitiveness nonetheless.

16 Robert Nozick, *Anarchy, State and Utopia* (New York: Basic Books 1974), 42–3.

17 Ibid., 44–5.

18 Peter Singer, "The Right to be Rich or Poor," in *Reading Nozick*, ed. Jeffrey Paul (Totowa: Rowman & Littlefield 1981), 51.

19 "We may define self-respect (or self-esteem) as having two aspects. First of all ... it includes a person's sense of his own value, his secure conviction that his conception of the good, his plan of life, is worth carrying out. And second, self-respect implies a confidence in one's ability, so far as it is within one's power, to fulfill one's intentions." See John Rawls, *A Theory of Justice* (Cambridge, Mass.: Harvard University Press 1971), 440. Rawls's elaboration of the circumstances in which the first condition of self-respect are satisfied suggests that he may have something like what I call "self respect" in mind, but the definition does not make that clear. For it is obvious that a person's plan of life might have been foisted upon her through a process of socialization which offered negligible opportunity for choice, and her ability to carry out her intentions might be the outcome of similar processes. In those circumstances, there might be ample grounds for self-esteem, in the sense I specify, but there could be little reason for self-respect.

20 This example comes from Richard Arneson's "Freedom and Desire," *Canadian Journal of Philosophy* 15, no. 3 (1985): 437.

21 Charles Taylor, "What's Wrong with Negative Liberty," in *The Idea of Freedom*, ed. Alan Ryan (Oxford: Oxford University Press 1979), 183. Taylor wants to argue that though there is "a quantitative conception of freedom" which does not import any extrinsic criteria of value, this conception is, morally speaking, a "non-starter." My point is that such a conception is not even coherent.

22 Isaiah Berlin, *Four Essays on Liberty* (Oxford: Oxford University Press 1969), 130n.; see also Onora O'Neill, "The Most Extensive Liberty," *Proceedings of the Aristotelian Society* 79 (1979): 45–59.

CHAPTER THREE

1   John Dewey, *Experience and Education* (New York: Collier Books 1963), 48.
2   Charles Clark and P.S. Wilson, "On Children's Interests," *Educational Philosophy and Theory* 7, no. 2 (1975): 41–54.
3   John Dewey, *Democracy and Education* (New York: Macmillan 1916), 125.
4   R.F. Dearden, *The Philosophy of Primary Education* (London: Routledge & Kegan Paul 1968), 18–24.
5   P.H. Hirst and K.S. Peters, *The Logic of Education* (London: Routledge & Kegan Paul 1970), 37.
6   Dearden, *The Philosophy of Primary Education*, 22.
7   Ibid.; P.H. Hirst, *Knowledge and the Curriculum* (London: Routledge & Kegan Paul 1974), 17.
8   Hirst and Peters, *The Logic of Education*, 37.
9   J.P. White, *The Aims of Education Restated* (London: Routledge & Kegan Paul 1982), 5.
10 Ibid., 121–2.
11 Ibid., 33–4; and J.P. White, *Towards a Compulsory Curriculum* (London: Routledge & Kegan Paul 1973), 93.
12 White, *Towards a Compulsory Curriculum*, 26.
13 Ibid., 35.
14 Ibid., 69–72.
15 There is a further obscurity in White's prescriptions because he vacillates between "some understanding of the desire to engage in an activity" and "some understanding of the activity." This has been pointed out by Robin Barrow, who adds further confusion by maintaining that understanding the desire entails actually *having* the desire. I assume that White's considered position would be that understanding the desire is what is crucial because unless I can see some activity as a possible object of desire it does not exist for me as an option, and the opening of options is precisely what White's curriculum is supposed to

ensure. However, I can understand the addict's craving for heroin, and hence conceive of heroin as a possible object of desire, *without* having the desire for heroin; and precisely the same point can be made about the desires others have to engage in more respectable pursuits. If we are concerned with opening options for students, it is disastrous to suppose that we must try to inculcate the desire to engage in the various activities we teach, for that would be trying to *dictate* the options they take. Unfortunately, Barrow's confusion of understanding a desire and having a desire also seems to have entered White's thinking in a recent article. Cf. Robin Barrow, *Common Sense and the Curriculum* (London: Allen & Unwin 1976), 69; John White, "The Compulsory Curriculum and Beyond: A Reply to Peter Gardner," *Journal of Philosophy of Education* 19, no. 1 (1985): 133–4.

16 White, "The Compulsory Curriculum and Beyond."
17 John White, "Compulsion and the Curriculum," *British Journal of Educational Studies* 32, no. 2 (1984): 148–58.
18 White, "The Compulsory Curriculum and Beyond," 134.
19 White, *The Aims of Education Restated*, 39.
20 White, *Towards a Compulsory Curriculum*, 20. White abruptly moves here from claims about postreflective choice, and the kind of curriculum it requires, to the conclusion that such a curriculum would give the student "as much autonomy as possible later on."
21 White, *The Aims of Education Restated*, 56–7.
22 Ibid., 39.
23 White, *Towards a Compulsory Curriculum*, 25.
24 Michael Scriven, "Education for Survival" in Purpel *Curriculum and the Cultural Revolution*, ed. David E. Purpel and Maurice Belanger (Berkeley: McCutchan 1976), 167–202.

CHAPTER FOUR

1 See Ivan Illich, *Deschooling Society* (Harmondsworth: Penguin Books 1973); Everett Reimer, *School is Dead* (Harmondsworth: Penguin Books 1972); and Ian Lister, ed., *Deschooling* (Cambridge: Cambridge University Press 1974).
2 See Julia Rosenak, "Should Children be Subject to Paternalistic Restrictions on their Liberties?", *Journal of Philosophy of Education* 16, no. 1 (1982): 89–96; Peter Gardner, "Liberty and Compulsory Education" in *Of Liberty*, ed. A. Phillips Griffiths (Cambridge: Cambridge University Press 1983), 109–29; Roalnd Case, "Pulling the Plug on Appeals to Irrationality, Immaturity and Expediency" in *Philosophy of Education 1985*, ed. David Nyberg (Normal, Illinois: Philosophy of Education Society 1985), 445–59. I also did some hand-wringing of my

own in "Freedom and Schooling," *Journal of Philosophy of Education*
17, no. 1 (1983): 45-55.

3 For example, Illich, *Deschooling Society*, 32-56.
4 Paulo Freire, *Pedagogy of the Oppressed*, trans. Myra Bergman Romos
(Harmondsworth: Penguin Books 1972).
5 R.F. Dearden, *Problems in Primary Education* (London: Routledge &
Kegan Paul 1972), 66.
6 Ibid., 67.
7 Illich, *Deschooling Society*, 52.
8 Lister, ed., "The Whole Curriculum and the Hidden Curriculum," in
Deschooling, 93.
9 For example, Illich, *Deschooling Society*, 21-5.
10 Ibid., 45.
11 Ibid., 57-68.
12 J.S. Mill, *On Liberty* (Indianopolis: The Bobbs-Merrill Company
1976), 13.
13 Some scholars have maintained that despite Mill's claim that his argument relies exclusively on the principle of utility, he does adduce noncontingent values in his defense of liberty. I prefer to take Mill at his
word when he disclaims any support for his argument from sources
other than utility. Cf. ibid., 14; and C.L. Ten, *Mill on Liberty* (Oxford:
Oxford University Press 1980).
14 This cluster of ideas is to be found in a variety of sources, for example:
Joel Feinberg, "Legal Paternalism," *Canadian Journal of Philosophy*
1, no. 1 (1971): 105-24, reprinted in Joel Feinberg, *Rights, Justice, and
the Bounds of Liberty* (Princeton: Princeton University Press 1980),
110-24; John D. Hodson, *The Ethics of Legal Coercion* (Dordrecht: D.
Reidl Publishing Company 1983), 1-14, 43-52; Gerald Dworking,
"Paternalism," *Monist* 56, no. 1: 64-84.
15 Feinberg, *Rights, Justice, and the Bounds of Liberty*, x. Feinberg is
paraphrasing here his famous article. He notes that he now regards
his former position as completely opposed to paternalism. I find this
claim completely baffling.
16 Joel Feinberg, "The Child's Right to an Open Future," in *Whose
Child? Children's Rights, Parental Authority, and State Power*, ed.
William Aiken and Hugh LaFollette (Totowa: Littlefield, Adams &
Co. 1980), 140-51.
17 Mill, *On Liberty*, 13.
18 John Kleinig, "Mill, Children and Rights," *Educational Philosophy
and Theory* 8, no. 7 (1976): 1-16; and John Kleinig, *Philosophical
Issues in Education* (London: Croom Helm 1982), 197-9.
19 See Howard Cohen, *Equal Rights for Children* (Totowa: Littlefield,
Adams & Co. 1980), 52-5; Francis Schrag, "The Child's Status in the

158 Notes to pages 105-119

Democratic State," *Political Theory* 3 (1975): 441-57.

20 Joel Feinberg, "Noncoercive Exploitation," in *Paternalism*, ed. Rolf Sartorius (Minneapolis: University of Minnesota Press 1983), 201.

21 Gerald Dworkin, "Paternalism: Some Second Thoughts," in *Paternalism*, 107.

22 Dworkin, "Paternalism," *Monist* 56, no. 1: 64-84.

23 Other conceptions of autonomy might be employed in the case against paternalism, but so far as I can see these do not advance the cause of the antipaternalists. Nicholas Husak has examined the relation between paternalism and some notions of autonomy I have not considered, and his conclusions are much the same as mine. I highly recommend Husak's excellent article. See Douglas Husak, "Paternalism and Autonomy," *Philosophy and Public Affairs* 10, no. 1 (1981): 27-40.

24 Mill, *On Liberty*, 93.

25 For example, H.L.A. Hart, *Law, Liberty and Morality* (Stanford: Stanford University Press 1963), 32.

26 Mill, *On Liberty*, 102.

27 It is interesting to note that Mill himself does not use the word in presenting his argument.

28 In recent years various attempts have been made to extend the philosophical concept of paternalism to include new ranges of actions. These attempts purport to bring the concept into line with our ordinary understanding of paternalism. But a class of actions is one thing and an attitude quite another. See, for example, Bernard Gert and Charles Culver, "Paternalistic Behaviour," *Philosophy and Public Affairs* 6, no. 1 (1976): 45-57; and Dworkin, "Paternalism: Some Second Thoughts."

29 Feinberg, *Rights, Justice, and the Bounds of Liberty*, 110.

30 But it has received some attention. See Dworkin, "Paternalism," *Monist* 56, no. 1: 75-6; Donald H. Regan, "Freedom, Identity, and Commitment," in *Paternalism*, 113-16. Amy Gutmann has defended compulsory schooling on this basis in two interesting articles: "Children, Paternalism and Education: A Liberal Argument," *Philosophy and Public Affairs* 9, no. 4 (1980): 338-58 and "What's the Good of Going to School?" in *Utilitarianism and Beyond*, ed. Amartya Sen and Bernard Williams (Cambridge: Cambridge University Press 1982), 261-77.

31 Francis Schrag, "From Childhood to Adulthood: Assigning Rights and Responsibilities," in *Ethics and Educational Policy*, ed. Kenneth A. Strike and Kieran Egan (London: Routledge & Kegan Paul 1978), 69-71.

CHAPTER FIVE

1 Drew Christie's "Recent Calls for Economic Democracy," *Ethics* 95, no. 1 (1984): 112-28 is a useful recent survey of empirical and philosophical work on this topic.
2 R.S. Peters, *Ethics and Education* (London: Allen & Unwin 1966), 310-11.
3 A.S. Carson, "Control of the Curriculum: A Case for Teachers," *Journal of Curriculum Studies* 16, no. 1 (1984): 19; Peter Scrimshaw, "Should Schools be Participant Democracies?", in *Values and Authority in Schools*, ed. David Bridges and Peter Scrimshaw (London: Hodder and Staughton 1975), 62.
4 Peters, *Ethics and Education*, 295.
5 For example, Carole Pateman, *Participation and Democratic Theory* (Cambridge: Cambridge University Press 1970), 103-11.
6 For example, Kenneth Strike, *Liberty and Learning* (Oxford: Martin Robertson 1982), 165.
7 Eamonn Callan, "McLaughlin on Parental Rights," *Journal of Philosophy of Education* 19, no. 2 (1985): 111-18.
8 See Sharon Bishop, "Children, Autonomy and the Right to Self-Determination," in *Whose Child? Children's Rights, Parental Authority, and State Power*, ed. William Aiken and Hugh La Follette (Totowa: Littlefield, Adams & Co. 1980), 154-76.
9 Wiliam Ruddick, "Parents and Life Prospects," in *Having Children*, ed. William Ruddick and Onora O'Neill (Oxford: Oxford University Press 1979), 124-37; David Bridges, "Non-Paternalistic Arguments in Support of Parents Rights," *Journal of Philosophy of Education* 18, no. 2 (1984): 54-62; T.H. McLaughlin, "Religion, Upbringing and Liberal Values: A Rejoinder to Eamonn Callan," *Journal of Philosophy of Education* 19, no. 1 (1985): 119-27.
10 It has been argued, for instance, that a democratic state will maximize the likelihood of just legislative decisions being made. See William Nelson, *On Justifying Democracy* (London: Routledge & Kegan Paul 1980).
11 A right to participate in democratic government has been defended on the basis of the equal dignity of all persons. See Carl Cohen, *Democracy* (Athens, Georgia: University of Georgia Press 1971).
12 Scrimshaw, "Should Schools be Participant Democracies?", 62. Scrimshaw does make some telling points against the "teacher knows best" thesis later on. But if these points are telling, it is wrong to assume that a concern for competence will naturally lead to regimes dominated by teachers.
13 Colin Wringe, *Democracy, Schooling and Political Education* (London:

Allen & Unwin 1984), 78-9; Colin Wringe, *Children's Rights* (London: Routledge & Kegan Paul 1981), 128-9.

14 Wringe, *Democracy, Schooling and Political Education*, 77.

15 Wringe, *Children's Rights*, 80.

16 Ibid., 122.

17 Wringe, *Democracy, Schooling and Political Education*, 79.

18 Ibid., 77-8. See also Wringe, *Children's Rights*, 128.

19 Wringe, *Children's Rights*, 129.

20 Wringe does make another argument against student participation. It can be dealt with briefly because it has the disadvantage of being circular. "The adult members of schools are quite properly held responsible by the community at large for what happens to the children in them ... Yet teachers cannot be held responsible for the safety, good order and learning of children in schools if they have not the authority to give necessary instructions and apply whatever sanctions are necessary to ensure that they are carried out" (*Democracy, Schooling and Political Education*, 78).

But why are teachers and administrators rather than students "quite properly" held responsible for what currently happens at school? It is nothing to the point to answer that schools are places in which virtually all the important decisions are now made by teachers and administrators because an arrangement under which all responsibility devolves to these persons is only proper if all decisions *should* belong to them. In other words, the premise of Wringe's argument presupposes the propriety of the state of affairs which it is supposed to justify, and that, of course, vitiates the entire argument.

21 Strike, *Liberty and Learning*, 49.

22 See P.H. Hurst, *Knowledge and the Curriculum*, (London: Routledge & Kegan Paul 1974), 122.

23 Strike, *Liberty and Learning*, 17-53.

24 Dearden, *Problems in Primary Education*, (London: Routledge & Kegan Paul 1972), 66.

25 Peters, *Ethics and Education*, 37.

26 If I am right about this then a further argument against democratic schooling must be mistaken. Francis Dunlop has opposed the democratization of schools on the grounds that it would damage the kind of relationship between teachers and students which educational success presupposes. See Francis Dunlop, "On the Democratic Organization of Schools," *Cambridge Journal of Education* 9, no. 1 (1979): 43-54. But Dunlop's characterization of this relationship does not make sense in light of the interpenetration of educational ends and processes.

The task of the teacher, according to Dunlop, is not to indulge "the pupil's own naive wants and aspirations"; it is rather to transform desires and aspirations. Therefore, teachers properly display a "downward regard" for their pupils who in turn evince a reciprocal "upward regard." More precisely, the student should "trust his teachers beyond all reasons (since he has no 'criteria' by which to test them) and submit to their authority." This "obedient submission" will go against the grain of most children, at least during adolescence, though that, of course, is no reason not to inculcate that attitude.

The telling objection to Dunlop's argument is this: the relationship between teacher and students which he describes is symptomatic of utter educational failure. If it supports any conclusion about the government of schooling, it is the rather uninteresting thesis that democratic schooling will not work where there is utter educational failure. Suppose it is true that educational direction goes against the grain of most adolescents in a particular school and that they have no criteria to determine what is good teaching. If education is crucially a matter of coming to appreciate things of educational value – and Dunlop's emphasis upon the importance of transforming desires and aspirations would seem to indicate that he would agree – then most of these students are very far from being educated. And if educational ends and processes are connected in the manner I have suggested, then the many years of schooling these adolescents have endured have had little or nothing to do with the process of education. Dunlop's conception of the proper relationship between teachers and students may comfort those whose efforts to teach adolescents meet with indifference or hostility. Unfortunately, the comfort it may bring is only achieved by disguising the fact that if students are thoroughly untrustworthy at that stage of their schooling, this could only be because our attempts to educate them (if indeed that is what we have attempted) have been dismally unsuccessful.

27 Carson, "Control of the Curriculum: A Case for Teachers," 23–7.
28 Antony Flew, *Sociology, Equality and Education* (London: Macmillan 1976), 104.
29 The argument of this paragraph is deeply connected with a point Michael Waltzer has made. Waltzer points out that a special feature of democracies is the proneness of citizens to engage in vicarious decision-making with respect to the actions of elected representatives. They ask, "would I have decided as she did?," and so forth. These vicarious decisions play a central role in the life of democratic institutions by determining the pattern of voting, political contributions, demonstrations, and the like. I would merely add that there is surely a causal nexus in the other direction as well. If one could not influence the political process in any significant way, there would be little reason to engage in this vicarious decision-making and thereby learn

about the appropriate use of authority. See Michael Waltzer, "Political Decision-Making and Political Education," in *Political Theory and Political Education*, ed. Melvin Richter (Princeton: Princeton University Press 1980), 159–60.

30 Flew, *Sociology, Equality and Education*, 104.

31 Dunlop, "On the Democratic Organization of Schools," 47.

32 Aristotle, *Nicomachean Ethics*, trans. David Ross (Oxford: Oxford University Press 1980), 1103a32–b1.

33 Ibid., 1143b18–44a36.

34 Ibid., 1103a14–18.

35 It is very significant that Aristotle's one reference to attempts to edify the young through sheer moral argument is less than enthusiastic. He maintains that argument is unlikely to have inspiring effects except for those who are already deeply committed to virtue. Cf. ibid., 28, 270.

36 Carole Pateman, *Participation and Democratic Theory* (Cambridge: Cambridge University Press 1970), 42–4; 103–11.

37 Ibid., 28–9.

Index

Aristotle, 26, 43, 144-6
autonomy: and authenticity, 37; and choice, 26, 31-40, 75-6, 78-82, 106, 146-8; constitutive value of, 45-7; and freedom, 3, 7, 23-4, 48-55; and the good, 80-2; and independence of mind, 26, 39-40; and individuality, 20, 25, 97-8, 108; instrumental value of, 41; and interests, 29-30, 52, 59, 62-3, 74; intrinsic value of, 42-5; as a moral right, 105-6; and moral virtue, 45-6; and realism, 26, 30-9; and reflection, 30-1, 38-9, 78-82; and respect for persons, 25; and self-perception, 115; and self-respect, 46-7; and the unity of a life, 32-3

Berlin, Isaiah, 9-10, 16-18

Carson, A.S., 139
child-centred education, 3-6, 63-8, 73, 123
childhood, 103-5, 129-31

Clark, Charles, 61
compulsion: and curriculum, 71-82; distinguished from coercion, 99; and freedom, 19, 116; grounds for, 100-1

Dearden, R.F., 65-8, 91-2
democratic schooling: educational value of, 144-8; objections to student participation in, 129-37, 139-44, 148-9; possible role of community and parents in, 125-8; role of teachers in, 133-6
deschooling, 6, 89-100
Dewey, John, 6, 11-12, 29-30, 57, 64, 68
discipline, 135-6
Dunlop, Francis, 143
Dworkin, Gerald, 106
Dworkin, Ronald, 21

Feinberg, Joel, 19, 102-3, 105-6, 110
Flew, Antony, 139, 141
Foucault, Michel, 135
freedom: value of, 23-4, 48-55; and constraint, 12-19; instrumental value of, 20-3; intrinsic

value of, 22-3; and knowledge, 58-61, 70-1, 76-8; negative and positive concepts of, 9-12; as open options, 19; and opposing value judgments, 8-9, 19; presumptive principle of, 22, 50-5, 112; quantification of, 50-2; and religion, 19, 22, 50-4, 74; of speech and assembly, 54. *See also* autonomy
Freire, Paulo, 90-3, 95, 137

Gaita, Raimond, 30

Haksar, Vinit, 21
Hart, Herbert L.A., 135
Hirst, Paul H., 5, 65, 67-8

Illich, Ivan, 88-9, 97-8, 100, 108, 137
interests: and choice, 31-2; and desires, 27, 64; and likings, 27, 30; originating new, 66-7; psychological and normative concepts of, 26-27; pursuing and developing, 61-3. *See also* autonomy